Political Thought
in
Ancient India

Reconstructing Indian History & Culture
(ISSN 0971-3824)

1. Society in Ancient India; by Sures Chandra Banerji
3. Early Indian Historical Tradition and Archaeology; by G.P. Singh
4. Vasantotsava: The Spring Festivals of India; by Leona M. Anderson
5. Ecological Readings in the Veda; by M. Vannucci
6. Vṛndāvana in Vaiṣṇava Literature; by Maura Corcoran
7. Social History of the Tamils (1707-1947); by P. Subramanian
8. Ancient Indian Coinage; by Rekha Jain
9. Buddhism and Socio-Economic Life of Eastern India; by Bimal Chandra Mohapatra
10. Chandragupta Maurya; by P.L. Bhargava
11. Mṛtyu: Concept of Death in Indian Traditions; by Gian Giuseppe Filippi
12. Yama: The Glorious Lord of the Other World; by Kusum P. Merh
13. Sacred Complex of Ujjain; by D.K. Samanta
14. Vedic View of the Earth; by S.R.N. Murthy
15. Society in the Atharvaveda; by B.S. Kharade
16. Orissan History, Culture and Archaeology; by S. Pradhan
17. Education in Ancient India; by Mitali Chatterjee
18. Surā: The Liquor and the Vedic Sacrifice; by M.B. Kolhatkar
19. Human Ecology in the Vedas; by Marta Vannucci
20. Governance in Ancient India; by Anupa Chandra Pandey
21. The Cultural Glory of Ancient India: A Literary Overview; by Sures Chandra Banerji
22. Kauṭilya's Arthaśāstra in the Light of Modern Science & Technology; by Sunil Sen Sarma
23. History of Jainism: With Special Reference to Mathurā; by V.K. Sharma
24. Cultural Tourism in India: Museums, Monuments & Arts: Theory and Practice; by S.P. Gupta; Krishna Lal; Mahua Bhattacharya
25. Ancient Indian Historiography: Sources and Interpretations; by G.P. Singh
26. Republics, Kingdoms, Towns and Cities in Ancient India; by G.P. Singh
27. Facets of Ancient Indian History and Culture: New Perception; by G.P. Singh
28. Kamakhya: A Socio-cultural Study; by Nihar Ranjan Mishra
29. History and Culture of Tamil Nadu as Gleaned from the Sanskrit Inscriptions (Vol. 1) (up to c. AD 1310); by Chithra Madhavan
30. Lifestyle of the Vedic People; by Pranati Ghosal
31. History and Culture of Tamil Nadu as Gleaned from the Sanskrit Inscriptions (Vol. 2) (up to c. AD 1310 - c. 1885 AD); by Chithra Madhavan
32. Matrimonial Alliances and Ancient Indian Polity (c. 600 BCE to c. 650); by Preeti Prabhat
33. Artisans and Craftsmen of Northern India; by Kuldeep Singh Thind
34. The Evolution of Historiographical Tradition in Ancient and Medieval India; by G.P. Singh
35. Warfare in Ancient India: Theory and Practice; by Soma Basu
36. Sanskrit Education and Literature in Ancient and Medieval Tamil Nadu: An Epigraphical Study; by Chithra Madhavan
37. Rājadharma in Mahābhārata; by Priyanka Pandey
38. Interstate Relations in North India; by Shiva Bajpai

Reconstructing Indian History & Culture, no. 2

Political Thought in Ancient India

Emergence of the State, Evolution of Kingship and Inter-State Relations based on the Saptāṅga Theory of State

G.P. Singh
PhD, FRAS (London)

DK PRINTWORLD
Publishers of Indian Traditions

Cataloging in Publication Data — DK
[Courtesy: D.K. Agencies (P) Ltd. <docinfo@dkagencies.com>]

Singh, G. P., author.
Political thought in ancient India : emergence of the state, evolution of kingship, and inter-state relations based on the saptāṅga theory of state / G.P. Singh – Fourth impression.
pages cm. – (Reconstructing Indian history & culture, ISSN 0971-3824 ; no. 2)
Includes text in Sanskrit.
"First published in India in 1993"–Title page verso.
Includes bibliographical references and index.
ISBN 9788124600016 (HB)

1. Political science–India–History. 2. State, The. 3. India–Politics and government–To 997. I. Title. II. Series: Reconstructing Indian history & culture, ISSN 0971-3824 ; no. 2.

LCC JC50.S56 2025 | DDC 320.954 23

ISBN 978-81-246-0001-6
First Published in India in 1993
Reprinted in 2005, 2019
Fourth impression published in 2025

Printed and published by:
D.K. Printworld (P) Ltd.
Regd. office : "*Vedaśrī*," F-395, Sudarshan Park
(Metro Station: ESI Hospital), New Delhi - 110015
Phones : (011) 4172 2626, 98713 94815
e-mail : indology@dkprintworld.com
Web : www.dkprintworld.com

PREFACE

THE present work primarily deals with the emergence of the State, evolution of kingship and inter-state relations in ancient India. These are some of the important aspects of ancient Indian polity. The details of the subject provided in the body of this volume are entirely based on the *Saptāṅga* theory of State, as propounded by ancient Indian political thinkers of different ages in their respective works.

The work is, by and large, based on the original sources (texts, translations and commentaries). In this regard mention may first be made of the *Śānti-Parvan* (*Rājadharma* Section) of the *Mahābhārata*, which is the earliest valuable semi-historical record on *Rājyaśāstra* or the science of polity. The text concerned provides an exhaustive and trustworthy account of the origin and evolution of the state and kingship, inter-state relations, etc. The data contained in the *Āsramavāsikaparvan* of the *Mahābhārata* are also of considerable historical importance. Like the *Mahābhārata*, the *Purāṇas* – the *Matsya, Agni, Padma* (*Svarga- khaṇḍa*) and *Viṣṇudharmottara* also deal with the seven constituents (*svāmin, amātyas, janapada* or *rāṣṭra, durgas or pura, kosha, daṇḍa* or *bala* and *mitra*) of the state. This was the popular concept of the '*Saptāṅga Rājya*' in ancient India. The importance of these elements in the state formation process in early India has been highlighted in different sources in different ways.

The *Vedic* literature comprising the *Saṁhitās*—the *Ṛgveda, Atharvaveda* and *Yajurveda* and the *Brāhmaṇas—Aitareya*, Taittirīya and *Śatapatha*, and the *Vālmīki-Rāmāyaṇa* also throw light on some aspects of the subject relating to the evolution of the institution of kingship and theory and practice of government in the contemporary times.

The *Dharmasūtras* of Gautama, *Āpastamba, Baudhāyana* and *Vasiṣṭha* (*c.* 600-300 B.C.) and the *Dharmaśāstras*—the *Manu Smṛti* (written during the *Śunga* period, some time between *c.* 185-72 B.C.), the *Yājñavalkya* and *Viṣṇu Smṛtis* or *Viṣṇu Dharma-Sūtra* (*c.* 100-200 A.D.), the *Nārada* and *Bṛhaspati Smṛtis* (*c.* 200-400 A.D.) and *Saṁkha Smṛti* (*c.* 600-900 A.D.) are very helpful for dealing with different aspects of the subject. The *Manu Smṛti*, in particular, like *Kauṭilya's Arthaśāstra* is of inestimable value. The text contains the wealth of data on the subject concerned.

Among the '*Rājaśāstrapraṇetārah*' or the pioneers in the field of science of polity, the name of *Brahmā* (*Prajāpati*) stands the foremost. He was the first to prepare a comprehensive code (*Daṇḍanīti*), which has been referred to as '*Rājaśāstra*' in the *Śānti-Parvan* of the *Mahābhārata*. It comprised several chapters on the constituents of the state, kingship, etc. He is also stated to have been the first to touch upon *Dharma, Artha* and *Kāma* (called *Tribargaśāstra*). It was *Viśālāksha*, who abridged the '*Rajaśāstra*' of *Brahmā* into 1,000 chapters and christened it as '*Vaiśālaksha*'. The compartmentalization of the science of polity into the *Dharmaśāstra* and *Arthaśāstra* was a development of the later period. Actually, the *Rājyaśāstra, Rājadharma, Daṇḍanīti, Arthaśāstra* and and *Nītiśāstra*—all stand for the science of polity in ancient India. Indra, the son of Bāhudanti was the first to write a book on the *Arthaśāstra*, which was popularly known as the *Bāhudaṅtaka*. The famous *Arthaśāstra* of Bṛhaspati, called the *Bārhaspatya Arthaśāstra*, which Vātsyāyana (*c.* 300 A.D.) has referred to in his '*Kāmasūtra*' (1.17), became the source of inspiration for many writers of *Arthaśāstra* of the later period. The name of Bṛhaspati also figures in the *Ait. Br.* (8.26). The *Śānti-Parvan* of the *Mahābhārata*, *Yājñavalkya Smṛti Kāmandakīya Nītisāra* and *Kauṭilya's Arthaśāstra* also testify to the fact that he was one of the authors of *Arthaśāstra*. The '*Bṛhaspati Sūtra*' available in the present form and ascribed to the ninth to tenth century A.D. is believed to be the recension of the ancient text. It was Dr. F.W. Thomas, who edited and published it (Lahore, 1921). It was Bṛhaspati from whom Indra learnt the first lesson of *Arthaśāstra*. The political thoughts of Uśana (or Uśanas), the author of *Arthaśāstra*, have been highlighted in the *Śānti-Parvan* of the *Mahābhārata*, the *Kumāra-Sambhava* (3.6) of Kālidāsa (the first century B.C.) and the *Matsya Purāṇa* (252.3). The work of Uśana has been referred to as the '*Daṇḍanītiśāstra*' in the *Mudrārākṣasa* (1.7) of Viśākha Datta (placed between the fifth and sixth century A.D.). It was Uśana, who abridged the *Bārhaspatya Arthaśāstra*, which originally consisted of three thousand chapters. The text is not available, but it is generally believed that the *Śukra-Nītisāra* was largely based on Uśana's *Daṇḍa-nītiśāstra* or *Arthaśāstra*. The *Arthaśāstra* of Piśuna or Nārada was known as '*Nāradiya-Arthaśāstra*'. Several verses have been quoted from the text in the *Vālmīki-Rāmāyaṇa* (*Ayodhya-Kāṇḍa*, ch. 100) and the *Mahābhārata*. Bhāradvāja, son of Bṛhaspati, was also authority on *Rājaśāstra* and *Arthaśāstra*. Kauṇapa-danta (identified with Bhiṣma) and Vātavyādhi (or Uddhava) also expounded their political theories in their works on *Arthaśāstra*. Dirghacārāyana, the friend of Pradyōta-Mahāsena and the preceptor of his son Pālaka of the Pradyōta dynasty of Avanti, also belonged to the same tradition.

It seems that the composition of works on the *Arthaśāstra* had begun after *Kalpasūtras* (*c.* 700 B.C.) and, particularly after *Baudhāyana-Dharmasūtra* (500 B.C.). From the study of the *Jātaka* records (compiled between the fifth and second century B.C.), it appears that by *c.* 600 or 500 B.C. the *Arthaśāstra* had got its recognition as a chief work on the science of politics. By the end of about *c.* 200 B.C., which nearly marked the end of the *Sūtra* period, the *Arthaśāstra* had emerged as an authentic work on *Rājanītiśāstra*.

It is worthy of note that the names of some noted early political thinkers like Viśālāksha, Bṛhaspati, Prāchetas, Manu, Uśana, Bhāradvāja, etc. have been mentioned in the *Śānti-Parvan* (Chs. 57-59 and 116-118) of the *Mahābhārata*.

Out of the eighteen *Ācāryas*, who were authorities on the *Arthaśāstra* and precursors or forerunners of Kauṭilya, the names of fourteen, *viz.* Viśālāksha, Indra (son of Bāhudanti), Bṛhaspati, Śukra (popularly known as Śukrācārya), Manu, Bhāradvāja, Gauraśiras, Parāśara, Piśuna, Kauṇapadanta, Vātavyādhi, Ghotamukha, Kātyāyana and Chārāyana figure in his *Arthaśāstra* (1.7; 1.15; 1.16; 5.6; 8, 1 and 3; 12.1). Their views, as quoted by Kauṭilya, have also been highlighted in the present work.

The *Arthaśāstra* of Kauṭilya (also known as Viṣṇugupta, and Cāṇakya being the son of Canaka), which is one of the most important sources of our information about the subject under review, deserves special mention here. Its antiquity and authorship have always been the subject of controversy among the scholars. The evidences adduced in the text itself (*Arthaśāstra*, 15, 1, last but one verse) and *Kāmandakīya-Nītisāra* (4, 5, 7) and *Daśakumāracarita* (*Ucchavāsa* 8) of Daṇḍin (*c*. 500-650 A.D.) confirm the truth that the *Arthaśāstra* was originally composed by Kauṭilya, who overthrew the Nanda dynasty and installed Candragupta Maurya (*c*. 321-297 B.C.) on the throne of Magadha. Pt. Shamaśāstri, Pt. Ganapatiśāstri, N.N. Law, K.P. Jayaswal, Radhakumud Mukherji, R.G. Bhandarkar, Jayachandra Vidyalankar, V.A. Smith, H. Jacobi, Fleet, Hillebrandt and others support the view in favour of its composition by the minister of Candragupta Maurya. The views of J. Jolly, Winternitz and A.B. Keith, that the text concerned does not belong to Kauṭilya; the historical authenticity of its author can be doubted; it was not written earlier than the third century A.D. and it is not authentic one, appear to be fanciful, and hence, they can be dismissed. In fact, Kauṭilya's *Arthaśāstra* (a manifestation of *Nītiśāstra* and

Daṇḍanīti) consisting of six-thousand verses was composed for Candragupta Maurya around *c*. 300 B.C. K.P. Jayaswal's statement (*Hindu Polity*, Bangalore, 1981, App. C, Notes, p. 374), that it was written in the 4th century B.C., is perfectly valid.

The political ideas of Kauṭilya expounded in his *Arthaśāstra* profoundly influenced the writings of subsequent period extending from the time of Kālidāsa (first century B.C.) down to the time of Bāna (seventh century A.D.), including Manu, Yājñavalkya, Vātsyāyana and Viśākhadatta. The *Yājñavalkya Smṛti* (*c*. 150 A.D.), in particular, bears the stamp of Kauṭilya's influence. The *Matsya* and *Agni Purāṇas* (*c*. 600-800 A.D.) contain a lot of materials identical with what we find in the *Arthaśāstra*.

The *Nītisāra* of Kāmandaka (also known as *Kāmandakīya-Nītisāra*) greatly based on *Kauṭilya's Arthaśāstra* and believed to be a recension of *Śukra-Nītisāra* was composed probably about 400 A.D. in the Gupta age during the reign of Candragupta II (*c*. 375-414 A.D.), as it appears from the opening verse of the text, and not in the eighth century A.D., as held by Jolly and Winternitz (Jolly, *Arthaśāstra of Kauṭilya*, Lahore, 1923, p. 46).

It is very difficult to determine the exact date of composition of the original *Śukra-Nītisāra* for manifold reasons. Divergent views are held by the scholars about its date. In all probability, it was written in the pre-Christian era. As Śukra flourished anterior to Kauṭilya, we may reasonably infer that he might have composed his *Nītisāra* sometime before the fourth century B.C. But on the basis of the evidence, as furnished in the text itself (*Śuk. Nīti.*, 2, vv. 361-69), one may ascribe it to the post-Śunga period. The text saw its several recensions between the fifth and the eighth century A.D. and then again between the eighth and the twelfth century A.D., which does not mean that it was originally written between the eighth and the twelfth century A.D. or between 1200 and 1600 A.D., as erroneously supposed by some scholars. Whatever may be the fact, the importance of *Kāmandaka-Nītisāra* and *Śukra-Nītisāra* as two valuable authoritative works on the subject to be dealt with here cannot be denied.

It is curious to note that the *Amarakośa* of Amarasiṁha (ascribed to the sixth century A.D.) also deals with the *Saptāṅga* theory of state, but the information supplied therein is very scanty. However, we have found them of some use for our purpose.

Apart from the works mentioned above, some other Sanskrit texts like the *Raghuvaṃśa* and *Mālavikāgnimitra* of Kālidāsa, *Abhilaṣitārtha-Cintāmani* (first four chapters) of Someśvara and *Mānasollāsa* of the Chālukya king Someśvara Deva (*c.* 1127-1138 A.D.), the Buddhist texts, *Dīgha Nikāya* (*c.* 450 B.C.), and the *Jātakas*, and the Jain works, the *Ādi Purāna* of Jināsena Sūri (ninth century A.D.) and *Nītivākyāmṛta* of Somadeva Sūri (tenth century A.D. and different from Somadeva of the eleventh century A.D. of Kashmir, the author of *Kathāsaritsāgara*), have also been found very useful for throwing side-light on the subject. The *Nītivākyāmṛta* is very often ascribed to *c.* 959 A.D. The accounts of classical historians like Megasthenes and Arrian, and others dealing with the invasion of Alexander the Great, are very valuable for getting a glimpse into the types of state, nature and functions of the state, etc. The epigraphic evidence has been cited in confirmation of the statements recorded in the literary and other sources.

The contributions made by Bhāsyakāras (or commentators) and Nibandhakāras on *Dharmaśāstra* and *Rājanītiśāstra* in the medieval period (*c.* 1100-1650 A.D.) to the enrichment of our knowledge about the subject have been widely acknowledged. Some of the important works of this class are *Rājanītikalpataru* (a commentary on *Saṁkha-Likhit Dharma-Sūtra*) of Lakshmidhara (*c.* 1100-50 A.D.), minister of Kanauja prince Govindachandra, the commentary on *Yājñavalkya Smṛti* by Aprārka or Aprāḍitya, (*c.* 1100-1130 A.D.), a *Śilāhāra* king of Northern Konkan, *Rājanīti-Ratnākar* of Chandeśvara (*c.* 1300-1370 A.D.) of Mithila School of *Nibandhakāras* on *Dharmaśāstra*, *Rājanītimayūkha* of a *Nibandhakār*, Nilakaṇṭha (c. 1610-1645 A.D.), and *Rājanīti- prakāśa*, one of the twelve sections of the famous work, *Viramitrodaya* (a commentary on *Yājñavalkya Smṛti*), of a commentator, Mitra Misra (*c.* 1610-50 A.D.).

It is undeniable that quite a good number of scholars have already dealt with the subject in the past and I owe a debt of gratitude to them, but still we find some scope to throw new light on some of its aspects on the basis of the data contained in some original sources. The bearings of ancient Indian political thoughts on the modern political theories and international diplomacy have been focussed here in detail. I am conscious of limitation of my knowledge of the political ideas and institutions in ancient India, and it is for the competent authorities on subject to judge as to how far I have succeeded in my attempt to present the details within a moderate compass.

All the seven constituents of the state including the king and the allies are inter-related and they cannot be separated from each other. For making an integrated approach to the study of the subject and for presenting its coherent picture, all have been treated as separate parts of one organic whole. However, in order to give a fuller treatment to each part the work has been divided into several chapters.

This short treatise, which is a piece of research work, will serve, as I do hope, as a book of ready use and reference to both students (particularly of the post-graduate level) and scholars interested in the study of ancient Indian polity with reference to the state, kingship and inter-state relations. If the book is found of any use, I shall consider my labour amply rewarded. I am well aware of the defects in the presentation of the subject matter. I crave the readers' indulgence for all the errors which have crept into the book.

G.P. SINGH

CONTENTS

ABBREVIATIONS

Abhilaṣi.	*Abhilaṣitārthacintāmaṇi.*
Ād. Pu.	*Ādi Purāṇa.*
Agn.	*Agni Purāṇa.*
Ait. Br.	*Aitareya Brāhmaṇa.*
Amk.	*Amarakośa.*
Āp. Dh. Sū.	*Āpastamba Dharma-Sūtra.*
Arth.	*Arthaśāstra of Kauṭilya*, ed. with Hindi tr. by Vachaspati Gairola, Varanasi, 1984; ed. by R. Shama Sastry, Mysore, 1909; tr. by Shama Sastry, Bangalore, 1915.
Av. Sam.	*Atharvaveda Saṁhitā.*
Bau. Dh. Sū.	*Baudhāyana Dharma-Sūtra.*
Bau. Gr. Sū.	*Baudhāyana Gṛhya-Sūtra.*
Bhāg.	*Bhāgavata Purāṇa.*
Bhā. Sāv.	*Bhārata Sāvitrī.*
Bis.	*Bibliotheca Indica Series*, Asiatic Society, Calcutta.

Bṛh. Sm.	*Bṛhaspati Smṛti.*
Cor. Ins. Ind.	*Corpus Inscriptionum Indicarum.*
Daśk.	*Daśakumāracarita.*
DN.	*Dīgha Nikāya.*
Ep. Car.	*Epigraphia Carnatica.*
Ep. Ind.	*Epigraphia Indica.*
Gau. Dh. Sū.	*Gautama Dharma-Sūtra.*
HOS.	*Harvard Oriental Series.*
Hv.	*Harivaṁśa.*
IIAG.	*Invasion of India by Alexander the Great.*
Ind. Ant.	*Indian Antiquary*, Bombay.
JASB.	*Journal of the Asiatic Society of Bengal*, Calcutta.
Jāt.	*Jātaka.*
JBBRAS.	*Journal of the Bombay Branch of the Royal Asiatic Society.*
JBORS.	*Journal of the Bihar and Orissa Research Society*, Patna.
JRAS.	*Journal of the Royal Asiatic Society of Great Britain and Ireland*, London.
Kām. Nīti.	*Kāmandaka or Kāmandakīya Nītisāra.*
MAIMA.	*McCrindle's Ancient India* as described by Megasthenes and Arrian.

Mālv.	*Mālavikāgnimitra.*
Mānaso.	*Mānasollāsa.*
Manu.	*Manusmṛti with the 'Manvartha-Muktāvalī'* commentary of Kullūka Bhatta (1150-1300 A.D.) with the *'Maṇiprabhā'* Hindi commentary by Pt. H.G. Śāstri, ed. with Hindi tr., interpolated Verses, etc. by Pt. Gopala Śāstri Nene, Varanasi, 1970.
Mats.	*Matsya Purāṇa.*
Mbh.	*Mahābhārata*, ed. with Hindi tr. by Pt. Shreepāda Damodar Sātavalekar and Shrutishil Sharma, Pāradi (Gujarat), 1968-82.
Mkd.	*Mārkaṇḍeya Purāṇa.*
Nā. Sm.	*Nārada Smṛti.*
NVA.	*Nītivākyāmṛta.*
Pdm.	*Padma Purāṇa.*
PTS.	*Pāli Text Society*, London.
Raghu.	*Raghuvaṁśa.*
Rāj. pr.	*Rājanītiprakāśa*
Rājat.	*Rājataraṅgiṇī.*
RNM.	*Rājanīti-Mayūkha.*
RNR.	*Rājanīti-Ratnạkara.*
Ṛg. Saṁ.	*Ṛgveda Saṁhitā.*
Śat. Br.	*Śatapatha Brāhmaṇa.*

SBH.	*Sacred Books of the Hindus,* Allahabad.
SI.	*Select Inscriptions Bearing on Indian History and Civilization.*
Śṅ. Sm.	*Śaṁkha Smṛti.*
Śuk. Nīti.	*Śukra-Nītisāra.*
Tai. Br.	*Taittirīya Brāhmaṇa.*
Tai. Sam.	*Taittirīya Saṁhitā.*
TSS.	*Trivendrum Sanskrit Series.*
Twy.	Text of the White *Yajurveda.*
Vāj. Saṁ.	*Vājasaneyi-Saṁhitā.*
Vāl. Rām.	*Vālmīki-Rāmāyana.*
Vas. Dh. Sū.	*Vasiṣṭha Dharma-Sūtra.*
Vas. Sm.	*Vasiṣṭha Smṛti.*
V.E.	Vikrama Era.
Viṣ. Dh. Pu.	*Viṣṇudharmottara Purāṇa.*
Viṣ. Dh. Sū.	*Viṣṇu Dharma-Sūtra.*
Viṣ. Sm.	*Viṣṇu Smṛti.*
Vy.	*Vāyu Purāṇa.*
Yāj. Sm.	*Yājñavalkya Smṛti.*
Yv.	*Yajurveda.*

1

THE STATE (Rājya)

THE *Saptāṅga* theory, as propounded in the *Mahābhārata, Purāṇas, Dharmaśāstra, Nītiśāstra, Arthaśāstra* and a lexicon – *Amarakośa*, deals not only with the constituent elements of State, but also with different stages of its formation, its composition, nature, functions, inter-relations, growth and decline, etc.

The seven constituents of the ancient Indian State as described in the literary texts concerned are the following : (1) *Svāmīn* (king), (2) *amātyas* (ministers), (3) *janapada* or *rāṣṭra* (territory and the people), (4) *durgas* (forts) or *pura* (nagara or capital city), (5) *kosha* (treasury), (6) *daṇḍa* or *bala* (army) and (7) *mitra* (allies).[1] The state consisting of these seven limbs or *aṅgas* (also known as *prakṛtis*) was generally called the '*Saptāṅga Rājya*' (or '*Saptātmaka Rājyam*') in ancient times.

Ancient Indian political thinkers' conception of the state was largely based on the principle of an organic unity. They regarded the state as an organic whole like a human body and looked upon its constituent parts as its limbs. Śukra, while comparing the seven constituents of the state with the organs of the body, called the king as the head, ministers as eyes, friends as ears, the *kosha* as mouth, the army as mind, the *durgas* or fortified capital cities as hands and *rāṣṭra* as legs.[2] All the limbs of its body politic have been considered equally important and complementary to each other. A great emphasis has been laid upon their co-ordination and integration as a necessary factor for the existence, growth and proper functioning of the state. None of them could function independently. In fact, all the organs moved like the wheels of the Chariot of the State. Their equal importance, mutual inter-dependence and indispensability for the state (for being considered as a full-fledged state) have not only been focused in the *Rājadharma* section of the *Śānti parva*[3] of the *Mahābhārata*, but also in one of the *Purāṇas*,[4] *Kauṭilya's Arthaśāstra*,[5] *Manu-smṛti*[6] and *Kāmandakīya Nītisāra*[7]. All the seven elements constituted the wealth of the State.[8]

The seven constituents, as stated above, played an equal role in the formation of the state. The king and ministers constituted the central government, which exercised the sovereign powers. The king used to run the administration of the state in accordance with the advice of *amātyas*, who symbolize not only the body of ministers but other administrative staff too, constituting as a whole one functional group. The third constituent—*janapada* or territory (popularly known as *rāṣṭra*), which was considered as an essential element of the state, was necessary not only to facilitate the settlement of the population, but also to promote the economic prosperity of the state. All the subjects ruled by the king were made to settle within the territorial units of the state. Since the structure of *janapada* was heterogeneous in terms of the settlements of people representing diverse clans, castes and languages, the king had to be invested with supreme power to exercise control over its affairs for consolidating claims to territory and maintaining its cohesion in particular and law and order in general. The *Kosha* not only constituted the resources of the state but also its financial foundation. Forts (*durgas*), *pura* and *nagaras* including fortified capital city having both political and commercial base and armed forces (*bala*) were of vital importance from the point of view of repelling the aggressions of hostile forces and defending the territorial integrity and existence of the state. The allies or friends were necessary for making suitable alliances, so as to secure the balance of power. The whole system of inter-state relations in ancient India was predominantly based on the theories propounded by different political thinkers in this regard.

The four important constituent elements of the state, *viz.* (1) the king, (2) government, (3) territory and (4) population were also known to the *Sūtrakāras*.[9] On the basis of this evidence as well as other indirectly referring to the welfare of the people as pre-requisite condition for the existence of the state, the hitherto existing impression that population was not taken into account by ancient thinkers as one of the constituents of the state can be dispelled. Modern political thinkers have also postulated that the territory, population, government and sovereignty are the main constituent elements of the state. Ancient political thinking goes well in accord with modern one, of course, only to a certain extent.

The relative importance of the seven constituents of the state varies from thinker to thinker and age to age. Moreover, one of the guiding factors for judging their importance was the contemporary political situation. The king and ministers were considered in all ages the two main pillars of the superstructure of ancient Indian states. However, the king continued to hold his supreme position as evidenced by a number of authentic sources. The king played positive role both in the formation and preservation of the state. For the better understanding of the subject it will be proper to describe all the limbs of the state separately in serial order.

NOTES AND REFERENCES

1. *Mbh.*, XII (*Śānti Parva*, Pāradi, 1979-80), 57, 5; 59, 51; 69, 62-63; 308, 153-56; *Mats.* (Gorakhpur edn., 1985), 220, 19 :
स्वाम्यमात्यौ जनपदो दुर्गं दण्डस्तथैव च ।
कोषो मित्रं च धर्मज्ञ सप्तांङ्ग राज्यमुच्यते ॥
Agn. (text with Hindi tr. by Tārinīsha Jha and Ghanashyama Tripathi, Allahabad, 1985), 225, 11; 233, 12 and 239, 1 :
स्वाम्यमात्यौ जनपदा दुर्गो दण्डस्तथैव च ।
कोषो मित्रं च धर्मज्ञ सप्तांङ्ग राज्यमुच्यते ॥ 225, 11
स्वाम्यमात्यस्तथा दुर्गः कोषो दण्डस्तथैव च ।
मित्रं जनपदश्चैव राज्यं सप्तांङ्गमुच्यते ॥ 233, 12,
स्वाम्यमात्यश्च राष्ट्रं च दुर्गः कोषो बलं सुहृत् ।
परस्परोपकारीदं सप्ताङ्ग राज्यमुच्यते ॥239,1.
Pdm. (*Svargakhaṇḍa*, ed. Aśoka Chatterjee Sāstri, Varanasi, 1972), 38, 59-60 :
राज्ञा सप्तैव रक्ष्याणि तानि चैव निबोध मे ।
आत्मामात्याश्च कोषश्च दण्डा मित्राणि चैव हि ॥
तथा जनपदाश्चैव पुरं च मनुजर्षभ ।
एतत् सप्तात्मकं राजन् पारिपाल्यं प्रयत्नतः ॥

Arth.; 6.1 :
स्वाम्यमात्यजनपददुर्गकोशदण्ड मित्राणि प्रकृत्यः ।
Manu.; 9.294 :
स्वाम्यमात्यौ पुरं राष्ट्रं कोशदण्डौ सुहृत्तथा ।
सप्त प्रकृतयो ह्येताः सप्ताङ्ग राज्यमुच्यते ॥
Yāj.Sm.; (ed. with Hindi tr. by Ramasharma Ācārya, Bareli, 1980), Vol. 2, 1, 353. p. 73 :
स्वाम्यमात्यो जनोदुर्ग कोषो दण्डस्तथैव च ।
मित्राण्येताः प्रकत्यो राज्यं सप्तांगमुच्यते ॥
Viṣ. Dh. Sū., 3, 33 :
स्वाम्यमात्यदुर्गकोशदण्डराष्ट्रमित्राणि प्रकृतयः ॥
Kām. Nīti. (ed. T. Gaṇapati Śāstri, *TSS.*, Tribandrum, No. XIV, 1912), 1, 10, 16; 4, 1-2; 4.77 and 8.5; *Śuk. Nīti.* (ed. Jivānanda Vidyāsāgra Bhattacharya, Calcutta, 1890), 1, 61-62; 1, 122-4; *Viṣ. Dh. Pu.* (Venkateśvara Press, Bombay, 1912, 11.145, 3) also contains a list of seven constituents with *sama* and *dana* in place of *svāmin* and *amātya*.

The aforesaid seven constituents of the state have also been regarded as the '*prakṛtis*' by Kauṭilya, Manu, Yājñavalkya and others. The nomenclature and order of these seven elements of the state are not found uniform in the texts. *Janapada* is interchangeable with *jana* or *rāṣṭra*, *daṇḍa* with *bala* and *durga* with *pura*. Out of these seven constituent elements of the state, the king, the ministers and high officials (ratnins), forts (*puraḥ*) and resources (*bali*) are, of course, mentioned in the Vedic literature, but details in context of their relations to the state as well as their mutual relationship are not furnished.

For seven elements of the state see also a lexicon—*Amk.* (with '*Maṇiprabhā* Hindi Commentary' by commentator Pt. H.G. Śāstri, Banaras, 1957), 2, 8, 17 :
स्वाम्यमात्यसुहृतकोशराष्ट्रदुर्गबलानि च ।
राज्याङ्गानि प्रकृतयः पौराणां श्रणयोऽपि च ॥
The commentator (*Ibid.*, fn. 4 and 5, p. 269), considering *pur* or *nagara* or its inhabitants, i.e. *Paura*, as a separate organ,

concludes that the state had eight organs. But in all other texts *pur* has not been separated from *durgas* and both have been shown as one organ.

The epic (*Mbh.* XII, *Śānti Parva*, 121, 46 and 122, 8; XV, *Āshramavāsika Parva*, *Pāradi*, 1977, 9, 8) exceptionally refers to the eight organs of the state (*Aṣṭāṅga* or *Aṣṭātmaka Rājyam*), but nowhere the text refers to that particular eighth organ. The commentary of *Vādirāja* on *Āraṇyaka Parva* (critical note on 9.8, p. 151 *cf.* B.P. Roy, *Political ideas and institutions in the Mahābhārata*, Calcutta, 1975, pp. 97-98) refers to the guilds of the citizens as the eighth *Aṅga* of the state. Someśvaradeva (1127-1138 A.D.) in his *Abhilasi*. (ed. R. Shamasastry, Mysore, 1926, p. 3n) refers to the nine elements of the state adding *Pauras* and *Śrenis* to the seven limbs. See also B.B. Mishra, *Polity in the Agni Purāṇa*, (Calcutta, 1965), p. 27. The inclusion of town, people and guilds or the mercantile community among the components of the state as two separate elements does not appear to be logical, because the former constitutes the part of pura and the latter of *rāṣṭra*.

The epigraphic evidence (*Ep. Car.* V. Channarayapattana, 149, 1183 A.D.) also testifies to the truth that even the kingdoms of the later period also possesed all the seven elements.

2. *Śuk. Nīti.*, 1.61-62 :
   सप्ताङ्गमुच्यते राज्यं तत्र मूर्धा नृपः स्मृतः ।
   दृगामात्यः सुहृच्छोत्रं मुख कोशो बलं मनः ॥
   हस्तौ पादौ दुर्गराष्ट्रौ ।
3. *Chs.* 56-128.
4. *Agn.*; 239, 1.
   परस्परोपकारीदं सप्ताङ्ग राज्यमुच्चते ।
5. *Arth.*; VI, 1 :
   अखिर्जाः प्रकृतयः सप्तैता स्वगुणोदयाः ।
   उक्ताः प्रत्यङ्गभूतास्ताः प्रकृता राजसम्पदः ॥
6. *Manu.* IX; 296, 297.
   स्प्ताङ्गस्येह राजस्य विष्टब्धस्य त्रिदण्डवत् ।

अन्योन्यगुणवैशेस्यान्न किंचिदतिरिच्यते ॥
तेषु तेषु तु कृत्येषु तत्तदङ्ग विशिष्यते ।
येन यत्साध्यते कार्यं तत्तस्मिन् श्रेष्ठमुच्यते ॥

7. *Kām. Nīti.*; IV, 1 :
परस्परोपकारीदं सप्तांगं राज्यमुच्यते ।
8. *Arth.*; VI, 1 :
9. *Gau. Dh. Sū.*, 11, 1 (for the king) and 11, 5-8 (for the people); *Āp. Dh. Sū.*, 2, 6; 25, 10 (for *Amātyas*) and 2, 10; 25, 11 (for *Viṣaya, nagara* and *Grāma*).

2

THE KING (Svāmīn)

POLITICAL thinkers of ancient India are unanimous on this point that the role of the king in state formation process was, proportionately, more important than others. The king appears to be an embodiment of the state. In other words, the former symbolizes the latter. In the true sense of the term, the existence of one depended on the other.

The *Purāṇic* evidence goes to show that :

सप्ताङ्गस्यापि राजस्य मूलं स्वामी प्रकीर्तितः ।
तन्मूलत्वात् तथाङ्गनां स तु रक्ष्यः प्रयत्नतः ॥[1]

Thus, the king was not only the source of the origin of the state that consisted of seven organs, but also the chief among all its organs. Kauṭilya has gone to the extent of saying that :

राजा राज्यमिति प्रकृतिसंक्षेपः ।[2]
स्वामी च सम्पन्नः स्वसम्पद्भिः प्रकृतीः सम्पादयति ।
स्वयं यच्छीलस्तच्छीलाः प्रकृतयो भवन्ति ।
उत्थाने प्रमादे च तदायत्तत्वात् ।
तत्कूटस्थानीयो हि स्वामीति ।[3]

Thus, the king and the state epitomize the *prakṛtis* (the seven limbs). The king, according to him was the symbol of the state. The rise and fall of the *prakṛtis* very much depended on the king. Because, he happened to be the principal among the seven *prakṛtis* of the state. All the *prakṛtis* were guided and moulded by him. Śukrācārya puts it in different way. He says :

राज्यबृक्षस्य नपृतिमूलं स्कन्धाश्चमन्त्रिणः ।
शाखाः सेनाधिपाः सेनाः पल्लवाः कुसुमानि च ।
प्रजाः फलानि भूभागा बीजं भूमिः प्रकल्पिता ॥[4]

"The king is the root of the tree of state; the ministry is its trunk; the military chiefs are branches; the army are the leaves of the tree and the subjects are its flowers; prosperity of the country its fruits and the whole country the final seed." *Rājanītiprakāśa* (forming a part of *Vira-Mitrodaya Rāja-Nīti*, a commentary on *Yājñavalkya Smṛti*, ascribed to Mitra Mishra, A.D. 1610-1640) also highlights the importance of the king in *Saptāṅga Rājya* :

सप्ताङ्गस्यापि राजस्य मूलं स्वामि प्रकीर्तितः ।[5]

In the *Mahābhārata* it has been mentioned that :

राजा सप्तैव रक्ष्याणि तानि चापि निबोध मे ।
आत्मामात्यश्च कोशश्च दण्डो मित्राणि
चैव हि तथा जनपदश्चैव पुरं च कुरुनन्दन ।
एतत्सप्रात्मकं राज्यं परिपाल्यं प्रयत्नतः[6]

The king should make every possible efforts to protect himself, *mantri, kosha, daṇḍa, mitra, janapada* and *pura* – constituting the state ('*Saptātmaka Rājya*'). It has been further added that :

कोशं दण्डं च दुर्ग च सहायान्मन्त्रिणस्तथा ।
त्रृत्विक्पुरोहिताचार्यान्कीदृशान्वर्जयेन्नृपः[7]
सप्ताङ्गे यश्च ते राज्ये वैपरीत्यं समाचरेत्
गुरुर्वा यदि वा मित्रं प्रतिहन्तव्य एव सः[8]
राजानं प्रथमं विन्देत्ततो भार्या ततो धनम् ।
राजन्यसति लोकस्य कुतो भार्या कुतो धनम्
तद्राजन्राजसिंहानां नान्यो धर्मः सनातनः ।
ऋते रक्षां सुविस्पष्ठां रक्षा लोकस्य धारणम्[9]
राज्यं हि सुमहन्तन्त्रं दुर्धार्यमकृतात्मभिः ।
न शक्यं मृदुना वोढुमाघातस्थानमुत्तमम्
राज्यं सर्वामिषं नित्यमार्जवेनेह धार्यते ।
तस्मान्मिश्रेण सततं वर्तितव्यं युधिष्ठिर
यधप्यस्य विपत्तिः स्याद्रक्षमाणस्य वै प्रजाः ।
सोऽप्यस्य विपुलोः धर्म स्वंबृत्ता हि भूमिपा[10]

We find that it was not possible for the king to ignore his ministers and other advisers, friends, *rāṣṭra* or *janapada*, treasury, forts and army. He had to extend an equal treatment to all for maintaining the existence of the state. On the other hand, the people taking the king as the Supreme had to take all proper care of him, because in absence of a king it was not possible to ensure safety of all their belongings. And in return, a king aspiring to have the state had to protect his people, which was his sacred duty. The state was just like a machine, which could only be handled by a wise king. The state was meant for all and, hence, it was absolutely necessary to protect it by all means. In spite of all adverse circumstances, difficulties and dangers, it was obligatory on the part of the king to do everything possible for his subjects.

Some ancient thinkers are of the opinion that "*Svāmīn, amātyas, janapada, durgas, kosha*, army and friends"—all had to face the difficulties one after another. Their deviation from the right path, their deteriorating conditions, fall, misuse, apathetic attitude towards welfare measures or their oppression by the hostile forces (called '*vyasaṅa*') were taken as detrimental to the existence of the state. It has been observed that :

स्वाम्यमात्यजनपदगुर्गकोशदण्डमित्रण्य-
सनानां पूर्व पूर्व गरीय इत्याचार्या:[11]

Manu, therefore, has rightly suggested that the king should pay maximum attention to the '*vyasaṅa*' of each one of seven *prakṛtis* of the state :

सप्तानां प्रकृतीनां तु राज्यस्यासां यथाक्रमम् ।
पूर्व पूर्व गुरुतरं जानियाद्व्यसनं महते ॥[12]

The king was, in fact, the pivot of the state. Kauṭilya has clearly stated that the king can appoint ministers, different officials and departmental heads or superintendents; he can dispel the cloud of misfortune befalling the *prakṛtis* (*amātyas*, army, *janapada*, *durga*, *kosha*, etc.); help them in case of any calamities, remove their difficulties and take them to the path of progress and can replace the *amātyas* with vices by virtuous one. He can influence them by his king-like qualities and take them into confidence. In his words :

मन्त्रिपुरोहितादिभृव्यवर्गमध्यक्षप्रचारं पुरुषद्रव्य-
प्रकृतिव्यसनप्रतीकारमेधनं च राजैव करोति ।
व्यसानेषु दामात्येषु अन्यानव्यसनिनः करोति ।
पूज्यपूजने दुस्यावग्रहे च नित्ययुर्क्तास्तष्ठति ।[13]

The king's own functioning in an arbitrary manner not only caused immense harm to his associates, but also led to the gradual decline of the state.[14]

For the materialization of the idea of well-organised state the existence of the king was felt necessary. There are different theories of the origin of institution of kingship. Some of those which became very popular can be briefly described here, so as to prove that the presence of the king was indispensable for the emergence of the state in ancient times. From the *Mahābhārata* (*udyogaparva*, 145, 23-33) it appears that the Kuru state, Hastināpur, remained for some time an *arājaka* state because of an absence of king after the death of king Vicitravirya, and the state, consequently, reached the brink of collapse.

The two different accounts furnished in the *Mahābhārata*, one about the divine origin of the king and the state and the other about the mutual contract between the king and the people for the appointment of a king, are very important for our purpose.

Bhiṣma, while narrating the story about the establishment of the institution of kingship and the origin of the king and the state in the *Kṛtayuga* (*Satayuga*) to Yudhiṣṭhira, revealed that in the dim past there was neither any king nor any state. There was no law (*daṇḍa*) nor was there anybody to enforce it (called '*dandakarttā*'). The people following the rule of *Dharma* (law) used to protect each other. Originally the people lived happily in the society and enjoyed peace and prosperity. But gradually the people began to forget their rights and duties. Their moral degeneration started. They became more and more greedy, selfish and wicked. The *Vedic* religion lost its sanctity. The state of anarchy and chaos and confusion brought untold misery to the people. The law of jungle began to prevail and, consequently, the strong devoured the weak as the bigger fish swallowed the smaller ones (called *mātsyanyāya*). Ultimately, the chief god *Brahmadeva* prepared a comprehensive code of law, called '*Nītiśāstra*', consisting of one lakh chapters and incorporating the details about the rise, growth and decline of the state. He is also said to have described therein the characteristic features of all the seven organs of the state with particular reference to *mantri, rāṣṭra*, forts, army and *kosha*. He appears to have included therein the duties, responsibilities and qualities of the king and his ministers, the ways and measures for protecting the state or *rāṣṭra* against enemy's attack, the rules of war and politics, the types of forts, the necessity of protecting the *Pur*, the duties of armed forces, *daṇḍanīti*, general rules for promoting the growth of the state, etc.[15] This was the first explanation of the different seven organs of the state, which was later developed and perfected, and eventually led to emergence of the concept of *Saptāṅga Rājya*.

After framing the code of law, Brahmadeva appointed Viraja as the first king. It was king Prithu, son of Vena (born in fifth generation of Viraja dynasty), during whose time the word '*Rājā*' for the first time came into being. And, thus, he established the supremacy of *Dharma* (the rule of law) on this earth.[16]

The word *Rājā* or *'Rāja'* originated from *'rañj*, i.e. to please the people. Prithu was the first king to please his subjects by protecting the law and maintaining an efficient government. The derivation of the word *'Rājā'* from *'rañj'* can be confirmed by different sources. In the *Vedic* text also it has been said :

सोऽरज्यत ततो राजन्योऽजायत ।[17]

Thus, he became known as *Rājan* or *Rājanya* because of pleasing his subjects. But according to Nirukta (2.3) the word *'Rājan'* is derivative of *'Rājā'*. The *Purāṇakāras* and other political thinkers have also accepted it. Kālidāsa also says :

"तथैव सोऽभूदन्वर्थो राजा प्रकृतिरञ्जनात्"[18]

Thus, Raghu assumed the office of *Rājā* because of pleasing his subjects.

From another account also, as contained in the epic, it is quite evident that the people were very eager to have a king for the sake of the state. There was general feeling that there can be no state without a king. In the kingless state there can be no guarantee of protection of life, property and *Dharma*. State without king will lead to an anarchy. According to the *Vedic* tradition, it was believed that it is not proper to live in a state or *Rāṣṭra* without a king. They took it as sin to live in such a state. They were convinced that the state without king and army will fall prey to the enemy. The king should be very strong and powerful. They were well aware of the fact that in the remote past the people living in the *'Arājaka Rājya'* ruined themselves by attacking each other because of an absence of a king. Thus, they entered into a mutual agreement for having a king for their own protection as well as for the creation of the state and its welfare. They all took vow to live peacefully. They appealed to *Brahmadeva*, the creator, to appoint a king to look after them and to put an end to the state of anarchy. The creator appointed Manu as their king. He first refused to accept this office, but after a lot of persuasion, ultimately, agreed to become their king. He was worshipped by the people and being surrounded by army he came out before the public. Thereafter, *Śaṅkha*, a *Smṛtikāra,* composed a *Śāstra* dealing with various subjects.

The above statements can be proved by the following evidence :

राष्ट्रस्यैतत्कृत्यतमं राज एवामिषेचनम्
अनिन्द्रमबलं राष्ट्रं दस्यवोऽभिभवन्ति च ॥
अराजकेषु राष्ट्रेषु धर्मो न व्यवतिष्ठते ।
परस्परं च खादन्ति सर्वथा धिगराजकम् ॥
इन्द्रमेनं प्रवृणुते यद्राजानमिति श्रुतिः ।
यथैवेन्द्रस्तथा राजा संपूज्यो भूतिमिच्छता ॥
नाराजकेषु राष्ट्रेषु वस्तव्यमिति वैदिकम ।
नाराजकेषु राष्ट्रेषु हव्यमग्निर्वहत्यपि ॥
अथ चेदभिवर्तेत राज्यार्थी बलवत्तरः ।
अराजकानि राष्ट्राणि हतराजानि वा पुनः ।
प्रत्युद्गभ्याभिपूज्यः स्यादेतदत्र सुमन्त्रितम् ।
न हि पापात्यापतरमस्ति किंचिदराजकात् ॥
स चेत्समनुपश्येत सभग्रं कुशलं भवेत् ।
बलवान्हि प्रकुपितः कुर्यान्त्रिःशेषतामपि ॥
तस्माद्राजैव कर्त्तव्यः सततं भूतिमिच्छता ।

न धनार्थो न दाशर्थस्तेषां येषामराजकम ॥
प्रीयते हि हरन्पाप: परवित्तमराजके ।
यदास्य उद्धरन्त्यन्ये तदा राजानमिच्छति ॥
पापा अपितदा क्षेमं न लभन्ते कदाचन ।
एकस्य हि द्वौ हरतो द्वयोश्च बहवोऽपरे ॥
अराजका: प्रजा: पूर्व विनेशुरिति नं श्रुतम् ।
परस्परं भक्षयन्तो मत्स्या इव जले कृशान ॥
ता: समेत्य ततश्चक्रु: समयानिति न: श्रुतम् ।
वक्क्रूरो दण्डपरुषो यश्च स्थात्पारदारिक: ।
यश्च नस्वमथादधात्त्याज्या नस्तादृशा इति
सहितास्तास्तदा जग्मुरसुखार्ता: पितामहम्
ऊनीश्वरा विनश्यामो भगवान्नीष्वरंदिश ॥
यं पूजयेम संभूय यश्च न: परिपालयेत् ।
ताभ्यो मनुं व्यादिदेश मनुर्नाभिननन्द ता: ॥
x x x x
स निर्ययौ महातेजा बलेन महता बृत: ।
महाभिजनसंपन्नस्तेजसा प्रज्वलन्निव ॥[19]

The epic accounts represent the synthesis of both the divine origin theory and social contract theory, so far as origins of kingship and state are concerned. Both the theories are more or less based on certain assumptions. But both contain some elements of truth. The idea of golden age prevailing in the primaeval antiquity (when the people were guided by the law of nature) underlying the first theory was also hinted at by Rousseau in the eighteenth century. The social contract theory propounded by ancient Indian thinkers was also advocated by Hobbes, Locke and Rousseau. Though the theories propounded by them are supposed to be manifestations of the progressive stage of political thinking, they find their roots in ancient Indian thinking. We do not find any positive evidence in the epic of the direct agreement between the king and the people imposing obligation on each other. Such contract was not possible in a society where there was, of course, some understanding between Manu as a king, on the one hand, and the people, on the other. Because, we find that the people while persuading the king to rule over them, promised to pay him 1⁄10th of their accumulated wealth and 1⁄50th of their animal husbandry and gold as taxes, so as to provide resources to him. This is also an expression of the agreement of the subjects with the king to be governed by him. The evidence cited below from *Mahābhārata* will bear witness to the fact :

> मनुरुवाचः—
> विभेमि कर्मणःक्रूराद्राज्यं हि भृशदुस्करम् ।
> विशेषतो मनुष्येषु मिथ्यावृन्तिषु नित्यदा ॥
> भीस्म उवाचः—
> तमब्रुवन्प्रजा मा भैः कर्मणैनो गमिस्यति ।
> पशूनामधिपञ्चाशद्धिरण्यस्य तथैव च ।
> धान्यस्य दशमं भागं दास्यामः कोशवर्धनम् ॥[20]

Whatever may be the truth, it cannot be denied that at the initial stage state was regarded more as a divine institution than man-made. However, after the emergence of the institution of kingship as a result of the mutual agreement between the king and the people, the other associates of the former came into existence and gave a new shape to the state. The king and the people always remained integrated as two inseparable parts of the machine of the state. This was the earliest phase of the experiment towards formation of the state. The importance of both the theories, in any case, cannot be dismissed as totally unworthy of credence.

The evidence furnished in the *Mahābhārata* can further be corroborated by other ancient accounts. According to the Buddhist account, *Mahajana-sammata* accepted the request of the people to put to an end the prevailing anarchy and confusion and thereupon the latter elected him to be their king and agreed to give him a part of their paddy in return for his services.[21] State was taken as a very important institution to maintain law and order in the society as well as the country.[22]

Kauṭilya has also incidentally mentioned that because of the prevalence of *Mātsya-Nyāya* or the law of jungle in the society the people elected Manu Vaivasvata as their king and consented to pay him the necessary taxes (one-sixth of their income).[23]

The divine theory of kingship also finds support in the *Mānava-Dharma śāstra*. It is said that the God created king to save the whole world from anarchy. The first two kings to obtain the state were Prithu and Manu. In this regard let us see what Manu himself says :

अराजके हि लोकेऽस्मिन्सर्वतो विद्रुते भयात् ।
रक्षार्थमस्य सर्वस्य राजानमसृजत्प्रभुः ॥
पृथुस्तु विनयाद्राज्यं प्राप्तवान्मनुरेव च ।[24]

In other *Smṛtis* also more or less the same theory has been propounded.[25] Śukra's statement is in perfect agreement with that of Manu, so far as the divine origin of the king[26] is concerned. It is said that the information supplied by him about the origin of the state is not very useful. "He recognises a quasi-divinity in the case of a virtuous king . . . he was not much inclined to believe in the theory of Golden Age or Social Contract.[27]

In the Jaina source also it has been stated that when chaos and confusion took the place of peace and harmony, government came into existence to restore law and order. Jinasena, ascribed to the ninth century, has pointed out that it was first *Tirthaṅkara, Rishabhanātha*, who created kings, officers, various castes and occupational groups.[28]

The statements made in the epic, *Arthaśāstra*, law books and in the Buddhist and Jain literature about the existence of stateless society governed by the "Natural Law" before the emergence of the state and the transition from "*Arājaka Rājya*" to a orderly state of society have been widely supported by different authorities[29] on the subject. There is no denying that the state was indispensable for the protection of the people as well as society. On the other hand, the creation of state through social contract for the establishment of the rule of law as well as for the sake of justice and security has also been supported by some.[30]

For providing equal justice to all the members of the society, for peace, progress and prosperity of the people, for the welfare of the state or *rāṣṭra*, for an efficient administration, to protect the weaker sections of society from stronger one, to punish the offender and finally to keep everyone within the limits of '*Dharma*', a '*Daṇḍa-nīti* '(law) was framed and the king also known as '*Daṇḍakartā*' or '*Daṇḍadhara*,' was invested with power to enforce it for the accomplishment of the goal. The primary objective behind such step was to do away with the then prevalent '*Mātsya-Nyāya*' in the society.[31]

There are, of course, some evidences to show that the king had divine elements in him.[32] But, on the other hand, there are some counter evidences to prove that those kings, who failed to perform his duties to the best of the satisfaction of the common people or did not uphold the rule of law or were immoral, corrupt, autocrat and tyrant, were either dethroned, deposed, killed or banished by his subjects. In some cases *Brāhmaṇs* and kings received an equal treatment from the people.[33]

In this regard there are some concrete evidences to show that those kings, who did not possess the leadership qualities, collected the taxes from their subjects without protecting them and did not look after the state properly, not only lost their states but also their lives :

मोहाद्राजा स्वराष्ट्रं यः कर्षयत्यनवेक्षया ।
सोऽचिराद भ्रश्यते राज्याज्जीविताष्च सबान्धवः ॥
शरीरकर्षणात्प्राणाः क्षीयन्ते प्राणिनां यथा ।
तथा राजामपि प्राणाः क्षीयन्ते राष्ट्रकर्षणात् ॥[34]
अरक्षितारं हर्तारं विलोप्तारमदायकम् ।
तं स्म राजकलिं हन्युः प्रजाः संभूत निर्धृणम ॥
अहं वो रक्षितेत्युक्त्वा यो न रक्षतिभूमिपः ।
स संहत्य निहन्तव्यः ष्वेव सोन्माद आतुरः ॥[35]

One of the kings, who was killed by his subjects, was that of Kalinga, who had appointed one barber as his chief *senāpati* (*Yaśastilakacampu*, 3, p. 431). Thus, it will not be correct to say that ancient Indian king enjoyed the divine rights. Several restrictions were imposed on him, so that he could not cause any harm to his subjects and steer the ship of the state along the right direction. Ancient India did not experience the divine rights, which were enjoyed in Europe in the sixteenth and seventeenth centuries, which witnessed the interference of religion in politics. The religion did interfere in ancient Indian politics too, but only for a considerable period of time. The interference of *Brāhmaṇs* in the administration, particularly in the *Vedic* and *Brāhmaṇic* periods, is, no doubt, a proven fact. Some references in the *Dharmaśāstras* and *Purāṇas* also adduce evidence to this effect. But, at the same time, this fact cannot be lost sight of that the existence of the political institutions, the established laws or '*Daṇḍa*' and the consciousness of the citizens did not permit the king to exercise his divine rights, as we find in the same category of literature. The relationship between the king and his subjects was mainly based on their mutual obligations towards the state. The clear picture about the processes of the formation of the state, different stages of its growth and about its nature will emerge only after we make the analyses of all the available data.

Before we proceed to do so, it will be profitable to put forth here the views of K.P. Jayaswal, who does not appear to be inclined to support the divine creation of kingship. In his words : "Divine theory of kingly origin and kingly right could have found soil in Hindu India if there had been no live interest and constitutional jealousy in the people to check such pernicious claims and notions. The Hindu theory of kingship was not permitted to degenerate into a divine imposture and profane autocracy. Jugglery in the divine name of the creator was not possible for the Hindu king as the race never allowed the craft of the priest to be united in the office of the Ruler . . . the matter of constitutional powers of the king, in fact, lay beyond the province of the ritualist and the priest. It lay in the hands of those through whose strength the king had become 'mighty' or vested with power. It lay in their Samiti, in the early period. In later times it lay in the equally important machinery – the *Paura* and *Janapada*.[36]

The kingship was also elective. The earliest evidence to this effect is found in the *Vedic Saṁhitās*. The king was elected by the representatives of the people, called *Viśas*, *Grāmini* (the head of the township or the village corporation or Chief of the village), *Rājakṛts* or king-makers, ministers and other popular officers of the state. The people elected the king to enable him to become the ruler of the *rāṣṭra* or state. They expressed the hope that the elected king may prove himself worthy of this honour. They also directed the said king to fulfil the wishes of the people, and to dedicate his life to the services of the *rāṣṭra*. The people also agreed to pay the tax, *bali*. The king was also re-elected or his restoration after expulsion was acceptable to the people.[37] The election was held in the Samiti. The *Kulapatis* and *Vispatis* played vital role in the election of king in the early *Vedic* period.

The *Brāhmaṇas* also provide valuable information in this regard. In the *Brāhmaṇa* period the king-makers (*rājakṛts*) were called '*Ratnins*'. They were not only the makers of kings but also creators of *rāṣṭra* (*rājya* or state) which was placed in the hand of a particular king :

रत्निनामेतानि हवींषि भवन्ति ।
एते वै राष्ट्रस्य प्रदातारः ॥[38]

The election of a king is supported by other evidence too.[39] In the later *Vedic* period the acceptance of leadership of a king by other kings was also of considerable importance.

Life began with '*Svarājya*', when there was neither any king nor any state. The people were *sovereign* rulers. But this state of affairs did not continue for a long time. *Gṛhapati* became the chief of the family. The assemblies were formed in the villages, *Samitis* (councils) were organised in the *janapadas* and above all *āmantraṇa pariṣad* or advisory council was constituted. The laws were framed and the concept of administration emerged. Thus the era of *prajāpati* ended and the era of kingship and state began. And ways and measures were devised for the protection of the people and for the growth of the state. This is indicative of evolutionary process, which followed in *Vedic* period. The truth contained in the above statements finds reflection in the following *Vedic* hymns :

विराड् वा इदभग्र आसीत् तस्या जातायाः ।
सर्वमबिभेदियमेवेदं भविष्यतीति ॥
सोदक्रामत् सा गार्हपत्ये न्यक्रामत् ।
गृहमेधी गृहपतिर्भवति य एवं वदे ॥
सोदक्रामत् सा साहवनीशे न्यक्रामत् ।
यन्त्यस्य देवा देवहूति प्रियो देवानां भवतिय एव वेद ॥
सोदक्रामत् सा सभायां न्यक्रामत् ।
यन्त्यस्य सभां सभ्यो भवति य एवं वेद ॥
सोदक्रामत् सा समितो न्यक्रामत् ।
यन्त्यस्य समितिं सामित्यो भवति य एवं वेद ॥

सोदक्रामत् सामन्त्रणे न्यक्रामत् ।
यन्त्यस्यामन्त्रणमामन्त्राणीयो भवति य एवं वेद ॥40
यदजः प्रथमं संबभूव स ह तत्स्वराज्यमियाय
यस्मान्नान्यत् परमस्ति भूतम् ॥41

The state, no doubt, came into being through the instrumentality of king. It will be wrong to say that state was a divine creation and not man made; and state originated only to bring the people on the right path.[42] It is the people who address to the king : "This state (*rāṣṭra*) is given to you. You are to maintain peace in the state, promote the well-being of the people and to increase the resources. You are meant for the prosperity of the people and for the growth and success of the state.[43] The king has also been called the public servant, who received taxes from the people in return for his assurances of their protection.[44]

K.P. Jayaswal's conclusion, that "(a) Hindu kingship was a human institution; (b) Hindu kingship was elective, the electorate being the whole people; (c) Hindu kingship was a contractual engagement; (d) Hindu kingship was an office of state, which had to work in co-operation with other offices of state; (e) Hindu kingship was a trust, the trust being the tending of the country to prosperity and growth; (f) Hindu kingship was expressly not arbitrary; (g) Hindu kingship was not above law but under it; and (h) Hindu kingship was primarily national and secondarily territorial",[45] seems to be valid.

The divinity of king is, no doubt, reflected in the *Vedas* and *Brāhmaṇas*[46], and later accepted by some of the *Purāṇas* and *Smṛtis*, but we should not be blind to the fact that this status was granted to the king by the people themselves in the *Vedic* period, so that his orders should be obeyed by the people for keeping the state machinery in order.[47] At the same time provision was also there to dethrone those kings who remained indifferent towards the people and the state. That is why, the contradiction is apparent in different texts. The duties and responsibilities of a king were of greater concern for the people than his powers and privileges. The doctrine of divinity, however, greatly influenced the administrative system of ancient India up to Gupta period.

Likewise, because of influence of *Brāhmaṇs* and priests on kings, which continued down to the end of the *Brāhmana* period, as we find some evidences in the *Vedas*,[48] *Brāhmanical* literature[49] and the *Dharma-sūtras*,[50] the state assumed the theocratic character, but after the fourth century B.C. the character of the state underwent significant change.

The actual process of the formation of the state began in the *Vedic* period. Because, we find that different types of kings and states, like *rājya*, *svarājya*, *bhaujya*, *vairājya*, *sāmrājya*, *mahārājya*, *ekarāts*, *adhirāts*, etc., which flourished in different parts of the country, figure in the *Vedic* literature.[51] The monarchical states were ruled by *rājā* (a king), *mahārājā* (a great king) and *samrāt* (an emperor). *Ekarāts* were sole rulers and *adhirāts* great rulers. The *rājya* denotes smaller kingdom; *svarājya* represents self rule or an independent state; *vairājya* was, probably, a kingless state or republic and *bhojas* were feudatories in nature. In Madhya-deśa kings and in Eastern India emperors were popular.

In the *Vedic* period the states were generally small.

The *Kuru-pañcālas* formed one composite state in Madhya-deśa or the *Gangā-Yamunā* doāb, which was ruled by a common king.[52] In the later *Vedic* period after the settlements of different tribes in different parts of the country, the notion of the territorial state or *rāṣṭra* generally evolved.[53] The king started ruling over both the people and the territory—(*rāṣṭra*) and not over the country.[54] As the time went on, different other states were formed at different periods. But according to *Saptāṅga* theory, we are concerned only with those states which were either controlled by the king himself or by other officials appointed by him.

In the epic age the different titles of the king were *Rājā, Bhoja, Samrāta, Kṣatriya, Bhupati, Nṛpati, Virāta,* etc.[55]

The coronation ceremonies further strengthened the position of kings in ancient India. It was after coronation that in the south the kings became known as *Bhoja*; in eastern India they were called *Samrāta*; in the west *Svarāta* and in the trans-Himalayan region (uttarakurus and uttaramadras) *Virāta*.[56] While making distinction between '*Dvairājya*' and '*Vairājya*', Kauṭilya deriving his authority from his predecessors, so-called *ācāryas* or '*Rājaśāstrapraṇetāraḥ*' explains that the former type of state was jointly ruled by two kings, while the latter was ruled by a conqueror. The former disintegrates because of the mutual rivalries and hostilities of two kings, while the latter thrives well provided the administration is carried out in accordance with the will of the people. But, on the other hand, he says that the former was ruled by the father and the son of two brothers under the guidance of *amātyas* and there was nothing wrong in it. And the latter was ruled by a conqueror from outside, who assuming that it was not his own state and he has forcibly occupied it does not bother much about the future of the state, collects texes from the people, tortures them and after confiscating everything he departs.[57] This explanation of Kauṭilya is a continuation of his discussion about the *Saptāṅga* theory of the state with reference to the king and the state.

Kauṭilya's views can also be corroborated by other statements. We find reference to the state of Avanti, jointly ruled (*Dvairājya*) by Vinda and Anuvinda, two brothers, in the *Mahābhārata*. Kālidāsa also refers to joint kingship of two sons of Agnimitra, named *Yajñasena* and *Mādhavasena*. A proposal was put forward to make both of them a common king to rule in the north and south of *Varadā* river.[58] The classical account provided by Diodorus also testifies to the fact that the state of Patala in Sindh, which emerged as city-state, was ruled by two hereditary rulers of two different dynasties, but the real power was vested in the council of the chiefs, as witnessed by Alexander himself in the fourth century B.C.[59] The administration of the state bears striking resemblance to that of Sparta of Greece. The details of procedures adopted for crowning the king after the creation of state are given in different sources.[60] Not only the king but also *yuvạrāja, māndalika, sāmanta* and *senāpati* were appointed.

The titles were conferred on the kings both in recognition of their services as well as according to the limits of the geographical boundary of the state, which were under their rule. This varied from time to time.

This also led to their gradation and categorization. Aśoka, whose empire extended from Afghanistan to the Bay of Bengal and in the south up to Mysore, was known only as *Rājā*. Khārvela of Kalinga has been called *Mahārāja* in the *Hāthigumphā* inscription. The Kuṣāṇa ruler Huviska called himself "*Mahārāja-rājadhirāja-devaputra*". Samudragupta was called only as *Mahārāja*. But other Gupta rulers called themselves *parama-devatā, paramabhattāraka, Mahārājadhirāja*, etc.

A noted *Nibandhakāra* on *Dharmaśāstra* or Hindu law, Candesvara of Tirhut (A.D. 1300-1370) in his *Rāja-Nīti-Ratnākara* has also referred to *Samrāta, Cakravartirājā, Adhiśvara* and *Mahārāja*. In ancient times the kings used to perform *rājasūya* and *asvamedha yajñas* for achieving the title of *Samrāta*. Pushyamitra, Khārvela, Vākāṭaka king, Pravarasena, Cālukya prince Pulakesina-I, Kadambas and many other kings performed the *asvamedha yajña*. The frontiers of the state of *Cakravarti* king were bounded on the north from the Himalaya to the sea covering the length of one thousand yojana (one yojana=4 krosa). In *Harṣacarita* Harsha has been extolled as ruler of seven *Cakravartis*. Māndhātā, Hariścandra, Purūravas, Bharata, etc. are known as *Cakravarti* kings. The different titles which emerged at different periods of history show the power and status of different kings as well as the nature of their states.

The system of election which was introduced in India as early as the age of the *Vedas* further continued in the post-*Vedic* times. This system also became a helpful factor in the growth of the institution of kingship. In the *Mahābhārata* it has been mentioned that after the death of *Parīkṣita* all the citizens of Hastināpur unanimously elected Janamejaya as a king, who ruled over the state with the help of his ministers and priests.[61] Kauṭilya also makes mention of election of the king (to be coronated) by the people.[62] In the early historical period too this practice continued. From Junāgarh rock inscription of Rudradāman (*c.* 150 A.D.) it distinctly appears that he was elected by the people of Saurāṣtra and after taking over the administration of the state he had taken oath to protect the people.[63] Harshavardhana (*c.* 606 A.D.) was elected after the death of Rājyavardhana by all the ministers led by their chief Bhandi and other officials. Gopāla (*c.* 750 A.D.), founder of the Gopāla dynasty, was also enthroned after being elected by the people. From the chronicle of Kashmir[64] we find several such examples. Yaśaskara was made king by the *Brāhmaṇs*. Baka was crowned after being elected by the citizens.[65] But Śuravarman after the exit of Utpala dynasty in 939 A.D. forcibly occupied the throne, but the *Brāhmaṇs* supported his claim.[66] When anarchy followed the death of Parameśvara Varman-II, a Pallava ruler, it was the people who elected the king. There are enough evidences to prove that the kingship continued to be elective in many ancient Indian states down to the eighth century A.D.[67]

However, this cannot be denied that the hereditary principle was also applied in succession of kings to the throne. Most of the kings inherited states through this process in both pre and post-Christian era, which can be substantiated by both literary and epigraphic evidences. It was exactly a hereditary monarchy. In general cases the kingship passed from the father to the son. In the *Vedic Saṁhitās*[68] and the *Brāhmaṇas*[69] such examples are found. Kauṭilya has also mentioned the same thing.[70] There is also a literary reference to succession of kings to the state continuously for ten generations through this process.[71] In the inscription of Khāravela (second century B.C.) there is a mention of coronation of one generation.[72] The division of a kingdom among different brothers has also been mentioned.[73] But some exceptions are also found to this. The *Mahābhārata* expressly states that in a state, which is conquered and the king is killed in a war, either his son or grandson or brother can succeed to the throne. In absence of either of them the daughter of the deceased king, if any, can become the ruler of her paternal state.[74] There are some instances in the Buddhist source to show that in absence of any successor the ministers and other high officials used to elect a person for the purpose concerned from amongst the kith and kin of the dead king.[75] Megasthenes has revealed that "when a failure of heirs occurred in the royal house, the Indians elected their sovereign on the principle of merit."[76] Kālidāsa says that after the death of the king Agnivarṇa, his wife (a widow) became queen and carried out the administration of the state with the help of ministers keeping in with the hereditary tradition.[77] The Jain tradition shows that a Jain Muni, Bhadrabahu, who was also known as Chandragupta Maurya, delegated the administration of the state to his son and himself went away towards forest, probably to undertake penance.[78]

According to Manu, the crowned king happened to be a *Kṣatriya* and he protected the people of the state according to the law and justice.[79] A person well equipped with the knowledge of the *Vedas* is worthy of being the chief of the state, chief of the army and chief of the judiciary.[80] We also find that the founder of some states belonged to the *Brāhmaṇa* dynasty. *Puṣyamitra*, the founder of Śungās rule, was a *Brāhmaṇa*.[81] In a period posterior to the Śungas, several *Brāhmaṇ* rulers belonging to the Kāṇvas, Vākāṭakas and Kadambas ruled over the state.

In most of the literary sources dealing with the *Saptāṇga* theory of the state as well as in other sources the qualities of a king and his rights and duties have been highlighted keeping in view the protection of the people and the welfare of state. The benevolence, magnanimity, the political wisdom, the sagacity, farsightedness, integrity, truthfulness, steadfastness, kindness, courage, etc. have been considered the virtues of a king. It has been emphasized again and again that he should protect the people, save the weak from being exploited by the strong, extend an equal treatment to *Brāhmaṇs*, *Kṣatriyas, Vaiśyas* and *Śudras*, have the knowledge of war, politics and diplomacy, uphold the *Dharma* or law, defend the state against hostile forces, enforce the *Daṇḍanīti* to curb the wrong-doers (because of inflicting the punishment on the wrong-doers the right of ownership came into existence), appoint faithful ministers, increase the resources of the state, take care of his forts, *nagaras, janapadas* and *rāṣṭra* and do all other things for all round progress of the people as well as the state.[82] The king has been called the protector of helpless, shelter for homeless and father of orphan.[83] It has been rightly observed that "when kings are unjust, even sugar and salt lose their flavour."[84]

All ancient political thinkers are of one opinion that the primary duty of the king is to protect his subjects by all means because the happiness of the former lies in the happiness of the latter. According to the *Mahābhārata*, the '*rājaśāstra*' (on polity and administration) lays great stress on this point "The protection of the people of whole state is the essence of *rājadharma*". This is what Bṛhaspati has stated.[85] Plato and Aristotle had also considered the happy life of the citizens as one of the ideals of the state. While explaining the details about the state and government to Vasumanā, king of Kosala, Bṛhaspati repeated the same thing. While elaborating he further observed that the king is indispensable for running the administration of the state and for the welfare of all the sections of the society. The social, cultural and economic development depends on the efficient administration of the state. The lawful preservation of the social customs and traditions rests on the protection of the state by the king. This has been categorically referred to as a testimony to ancient history.[86] Actually, the king has been called the root of the tree—represented by his subjects and, therefore, the progress and prosperity of the state fully depended on the king. The full details have been provided also in the *Purāṇic* literature.[87] It was indispensable for the king to have full knowledge of the six characteristic features of ancient Indian polity, one of which was the protection of his subjects. Manu,[88] Kauṭilya[89] and Kālidāsa[90] have also emphasized the same thing.

The king had to perform primarily four different kinds of function, *viz*. to protect and help all the citizens of the state, to maintain the rules of *Varṅāṣrama-dharma*, to punish the offenders and culprits according to the established laws or *Daṇḍa* and to dispense the justice. Besides, he had to defend the state against foreign aggression, to maintain peace in the state and to exercise his executive and legislative powers for smooth functioning of the state.[91]

One of the primary duties of the king was to keep his *Sāmantas* under control; this is what only Kauṭilya and Manu have discussed in connection with the theory concerned. Kauṭilya counts it as one of the parts of '*abhigāmika*' virtue of the king.[92] The explanations given by Manu in this regard are more satisfactory than that of Kauṭilya. According to him, the king should live in country, where *Sāmanta* chiefs have been subjugated.[93] Here it must be made clear that during the time of Manu (*c.* 200-100 B.C.) they were not like the feudal lords of the later period; rather, in his own words they were the people of neighbouring villages or areas, who, of course, settled the boundary disputes between the villagers.[94] They had to perform both political and non-political functions. The king had to suppress the hostile *Sāmantas* ("*duṣṭasāmanta*"); it was his '*āgneyavrata*'.[95] The *Sāmantas*—sentinels of frontiers—and other officials deputed by king to defend the state from enemies, if found helping the robbers by being neutral, were subjected to strict punishment.[96] It appears that their status was like that of feudatories, who had to obey king's orders, though they enjoyed considerable amount of freedom in the management of their internal affairs.

According to Śukrācārya, the annual income of one

Sāmanta (without putting the subjects to persecution) was from one to three lakhs *karṣa* (in silver) and that of *māndalika* four to ten lakhs *karṣa*, of the king eleven to twenty lakhs *karṣa*, of the *mahārāja* twenty-one to forty lakhs *karṣa*, of the *Samrāta* fifty-one lakhs to one crore, of the *Virāta* two to ten crores and of *Sārvabhauma* eleven to fifty crores.[97] There may be some exaggerations in the data concerned, but this fairly illustrates the distinction between the king, the *Sāmanta* and *Samrāta*.

A retrospect of what has been described so far gives us an impression that after the creation of the institution of kingship the state came into being. The king had to shoulder very heavy responsibilities towards the state. The position, status, powers, functions and privileges of the king varied from age to age. In the early *Vedic* period the powers of the king were very limited because the states were very small and tribal in character. But in the later *Vedic* phase the character of the state and powers of the king suddenly changed. The states became territorial in character and extensive in size, but, of course, not like that of the sixth century B.C. The powers of the *Kulapatis* and *Vispatis* decreased and the importance of the popular assemblies began to decline. And hence the powers and prestige of the king tended to increase. The use of the term *ekarāts, adhirāts, samrāts*, etc. in the *Vedic* literature shows that their position changed in proportion to the size of their respective states. During the period extending from the epic age to the times of Buddha different types of state were formed, which were ruled in different ways. The states of fairly extensive size began to emerge from the fourth century

B.C. onwards. The monarchy was hereditary in character. The state was generally ruled by an independent king, but in some cases two states were ruled jointly by a common king. Such states were called confederate states. In some of the republican or oligarchical states the chiefs or kings had to carry out the decision of the populace. The king in all cases had to protect the citizens of the state both against internal and external danger and had to run the administration of the state according to the prescribed *daṇḍa-nīti* and prevailing customs and traditions. He had to take care of all the constituents of the state by framing rules separately for each one of them. In all the ages the king, by and large, proved to be the backbone of the state.

NOTES AND REFERENCES

1. *Mats.*, 220, 20; see also *Agn.* 225, 12; *VIṣ. Dh. Pu.*, 11, 65, 21, 22.
2. *Arth.*, VIII, 2.
3. *Ibid.*, VIII, 1.
4. *Śuk. Nīti.*, V, 12.
5. *Vira-Mitrodaya*, p. 133. See ed. by Jivānanda Vidyā-Sāgara Bhattacharya, Cal. 1875; *Chaukhamba Sk. Series*, Varanasi, 1916.
6. *Mbh. Śānti Parva*, 69, 62-63.
7. *Ibid.* 60, 4.
8. *Ibid.*, 57, 5.
9. *Ibid.*, 57, 41-42.
10. *Ibid.*, 58, 21-23.
11. *Arth.*, VIII, 1. Kauṭilya's statement is based on the views of some *Ācāryas*.
12. *Ibid.*, IX, 295.
13. *Arth.*, VIII, 1.
14. *Śuk. Nīti.*, 2, 4.

15. *Mbh. Śānti Parva*, Ch. 59 :

नियतस्त्वं नरश्रेष्ठ शृणु सर्वमशेषतः।
यथा राज्यं समुत्पन्नमादौ कृतयुगेऽभवत् ॥13 ॥
नैव राज्यं न राजासीन्न दण्डो न च दाण्डिकः।
धर्मेणैव प्रजाः सर्वा रक्षन्ति च परस्परम् ॥14 ॥
पालयानास्तथान्योन्यं नरा धर्मेण भारत।
खेदं परममाजग्मुस्ततस्तान्मोह आविशत् ॥15 ॥
ते मोहवशमापन्ना मानवा मनुजर्षभ।
प्रतिपत्तिविमोहाच्च धर्मस्तेषामनीनशत् ॥16 ॥
न्ष्टायां प्रतिपत्तौ तु मोहवश्या नरास्तदा।
लोभ्स्य वशमापन्नाः सर्वे भारतसत्तम ॥17 ॥

x x x x

विप्लुते नरलोकेऽस्मिंस्ततो ब्रह्म ननाश ह।
नाशाष्च ब्रह्मणो राजन्धर्मो नाशमथागमत् ॥21 ॥
नेष्ट ब्रह्माणि धर्मे च देवास्त्रसमथागमन्।
ते त्रस्ता नरशार्दूल ब्रह्मणं शरणं ययुः ॥22 ॥

x x x x

ततोऽध्याय सहस्राणां शतं चक्रे स्वबुद्धिजम।
यत्र धर्मस्तथैवार्थः कामष्चैवानुवर्णितः ॥29 ॥

x x x x

अमात्यरक्षाप्रणिधी राजपुत्रस्य रक्षणम्।
चारश्च विविधोपायः प्राणिधिश्च पृथग्विधः ॥34 ॥

x x x x

मन्त्रश्च वर्णितः कृतस्नस्तथाभेदार्थ एव च।
विभ्रशश्चैव मन्त्रस्य सिद्धस्यसिद्धयोश्च यत्फलम् ॥36 ॥

x x x x

आसुरश्चैव विजयस्त्था कात्स्नर्येन वर्णितः।
लक्ष्णं पच्चवर्गस्य त्रिविधं चात्र वर्णितम ॥39 ॥

x x x x

तथा खातविधानं च योगसंचार एव च।
चौराटण्यबलैश्चोग्रैः परराष्ट्रस्य पीडनम् ॥48 ॥

x x x x

सप्ताङ्गस्य च राजस्य ह्यासवृद्धिसमञ्जसम ।
दूतसामर्थ्ययोगश्च राष्ट्रस्य च बिविर्धनम् ॥51 ॥
x x x x
रक्षणं चैव पौराणां स्वराष्ट्रस्य विवर्धनम् ।
मण्डलस्था च या चिन्ता राजन्द्वादशराजिका ॥60 ॥
See also *Ibid.*, *Vv.*18-20, 23-28, 30-33, 40-47, 52-69, 71-126; also V.S. Agrawala, *Bhā. Sāv.*, Vol. 3 (Delhi, 1968), pp. 48-54.

16. *Mbh. Śānti Parva*, 59, 127 :
तेन धर्मोत्तरश्चायं कृतो लोको महात्मना ।
रञ्जिताश्च प्रजाः स्र्वास्तेन राजेति शब्धते ॥
17. *Av. Saṁ.*, 15, 2, 8, 1.
18. *Raghu.* 4, 12.
19. *Mbh. Śānti Parva*, Ch. 67, *Vv.* 2-8, 12-14, 17-18, 20-21 and 29; see also V.S. Agrawala, *op. cit.*, pp. 67-69.
20. *Mbh. Śānti Parva*, 67, 22-23.
21. *DN.* (ed. by T.W. Rhys Davids and J.E. Carpenter, P.T.S. London, 1890-1911), Vol. III, pp. 84-96.
22. *Jāt.* (ed. by V. Fausboll, London, 1877-97; trans. by various scholars under the editorship of E.B. Cowell, Cambridge, 1895-1913), VI, pp. 39 f.
23. *Arth.*, 1, 13.
24. *Manu.,* VII, 3 and 42.
25. *Nā. Sṁ.* (ed. J. Jolly, Calcutta, 1885), 1, 1-2; *Bṛh. Sṁ.* (*Āndāśrama Skt. Series*, Poona, 1905; *Dharmaśāstra Saṁgraha*, ed. by J. Vidyāsāgara, Calcutta, 1876), 1, 1-16.
26. *Śuk. Nīti.* (ed. G. Oppert, Madras, 1882; also B.K. Sarkar, *SBH.*, Vol. XIII, Allahabad, 1914), 1, 71.
27. Altekar, A.S., *State and Government in Ancient India* (Delhi, 1977), p. 30.
28. *Ād. Pu.* (Banaras, 1951), III, pp. 30 ff.
29. Ghoshal, U.N., *A History of Indian Political Ideas* (Bombay, 1959), pp. 118-20; D.R. Bhandarkar, *Carmichael Lectures* (Calcutta, 1918-9), pp. 115-22; N.C. Bandopadhyaya, *Development of Hindu Polity and Political Theories*, (Calcutta, 1927), pp. 295-7; P.N. Banerjee *Public*

Administration in Ancient India, (London, 1916), pp. 34 f; Beni Prasad, *Theory of Govt. in Ancient India* (Allah., 1928), pp. 235-6; V.R.R. Dikshitar, *Hindu Administrative Institutions* (Madras, 1929), pp. 17-18; Altekar, *op. cit.*, pp. 26-31.

30. Gough, T.W., *The Social Contract*, p. 234.
31. For details see *Manu.*, VII, 13-34; *Mbh. Śānti Parva*, 15, 8, 30; 67, 16; *Agn.* 226-13-16; *Mats.*, 225, 1-10, 17; *Śat. Br.* (ed. A. Chinnaswami Śāstri & c. 2nd edn. Varanasi, 1984), 11.6.24; *Kām. Nīti.* (ed. by R. Mitra, *BIS.*, Calcutta, 1896), 1, 1; 2, 38-44; *Viṣ. Dh. Sū.*, 3, 95; *Yāj. Sm.* 1, 354; *Mānaso.* (of Somesvara Deva), 2, 16, 1295; *Arth.*, 1, 4; 5, 1; *Rāj. Pr.*, p. 30.
32. *Manu.*, VII, 4-8; IX, 303-5; *Mbh. Śānti Parva*, 68, 40; *Mats.* 226, 1, 9-12; *Agn.*, 226, 17-20; *Śuk. Nīti.*, 1, 71-79; *Mkd.* 24, 23-28; 27, 21-26; *Vy.*, 57, 72; *Viṣ. Dh. Pu.* (S. Kramrisch, Calcutta, 1928; P. Shah, Baroda, 1961), 2, 2, 9; *Gau. Dh. Sū.*, 11, 32; *Āp. Dh. Sū.*, 1, 11, 31, 5.
33. *Manu.*, VII, 27, 34, 111-112; 2, 27-28; *Mbh. Śānti Parva*, 59, 93-95; 92, 19; 12, 6, 9; 78, 36; *Bhāg.*, 4, 14; *Kām. Nīti.* 2, 38; *Tai. Sam.* (ed. Mahadeva Śāstri, Mysore, 1884; tr. A.B. Keith, "*The Veda of the Black Yajus School*", Hos. Ed. C.R. Lanman, XVIII & XIX, 1914, Delhi, 1967), 2, 3, 1; *Śat. Br.*, 12, 9, 3, 1 & 3; *Yāj. Sm.*, 1, 356; *Śuk. Nīti.*, 1, 70, 86-87; 2, 274-75; 4, 7, 332-33; *Nā. Sm., Prakirnaka*, 25; *Gau. Dh. Sū.* 11, 1, 7 & 8; *Rāj. Pr.*, pp. 17, 83; *Ait. Br.* (ed. S. Sāmaṣrami, Calcutta, 1895, tr. A.B. Keith, Hos., Vol. XXV, Cambridge, Mass., 1920, Delhi, 1971, ed. with tr. by M. Haug, 2 Vols., Bombay, 1863), 37, 5; 40, 1; *Gau. Dh. Sū.*, 8, 1; 11, 27.
34. *Manu.*, VII, 111-112.
35. *Mbh.* XIII, *Anuśāsana Parva* (*Pāradi*, 1978), 60, 19-20.
36. *Hindu Polity* (Bangalore, 1981), pt. II, p. 228.
37. *Ṛg. Saṁ.*, 10, 12, 173, 1-6; 10, 10, 124, 8; *Av. Sam.*, 3, 1, 3, 1-6; 3, 1, 4, 2; 3, 1, 5, 6-7; 6, 9, 87, 1-3.
38. *Tai. Br.* (ed. with Sāyana's Comm. by R. Mitra, 3 Vols. *BIS.*, Calcutta, 1855-70; ed. Sāmaśāstri, Mysore, 1921), 1, 7, 3; see also *Tai. Sam.*, 1, 8, 9.
39. *Ait. Br.*, 1, 14.

40. *Av. Saṁ.*, 8, 5, 10, 1-5, 8-13.
41. *Ibid.*, 10, 4, 7, 31.
42. Dreckmeier, Charles, *Kingship and Community in Early India* (Oxford, 1962), p. 245.
43. *Yv.* (ed. with tr. by R. Sharma Ācārya, Bareli, 1974), IX, 22. See also R.T.H. Griffith's tr. Twy. (Banaras, 1899, *The Chowkhamba Skt. Stud.* Vol. XCV, Varanasi, 1976).
44. *Bau. Dh. Sū.* (ed. by Chinnaswami Śāstri, Banaras, 1934), 1, 10, 1; *Śuk. Nīti.*, 1, 188; *Mbh. Śānti Parva*, 72, 10.
45. *Op. cit.*, pp. 211-12.
46. *Ṛg. Saṁ.*, 4, 42, 8-9; *Sat. Br.*, 5, 1.5, 14.
47. *Av. Sam.*, 6, 9, 87, 1-3; 6, 9, 88, 1-3.
48. *Ṛg. Saṁ.*, 4, 50, 7-9; *Vāj. Saṁ.* (ed. with Mahidhara's Comm. by A. Weber, Berlin, 1852; ed. Lakshman Śāstri, Bombay, 1894) and Yv., X, 17 and 28.
49. *Ait. Br.*, VI, 2, 1; VII, 5, 24; VIII, 9.
50. *Gau. Dh. Sū.*, 1.11.
51. *Ṛg. Saṁ.*, 8, 37, 3; 10, 128, 9; 1, 25.10; 2, 28, 6; 5, 85, 1; 6, 68, 9; 8, 92, 1; 7, 37, 3; 2, 28, 1; *Av. Sam.*; 3, 4, 1; 6, 98, 1; 9, 10, 24; *Ait. Br.* VIII, 2, 6; VIII, 3, 13-14.
52. *Ait. Br.*, VIII, 14.
53. *Av. Sam.*, III, 1, 4, 1-2; VI, 10, 98, 2-3; XIX, 4, 30, 3-4; XX, 9, 127, 9-10; *Ait. Br.*, VII, 3, 14.
54. *Tai. Saṁ.*, 11, 3, 3-4.
55. *Mbh. Śānti Parva*, 68, 54.
56. *Ait. Br.* 38.
57. *Arth.*, 8, 2.
58. *Mbh.*, V, *Udyoga Parva* (Pāradi, 1969), 19, 24; 163, 6; VII, *Drona Parva* (Pāradi, 1975), 52, 17; *Mālv.* (text with tr. by M.R. Kale revd. by J.L. Dave and S.A. Upadhyaya, Delhi, 1985), Act. V, V.13; pp. 188-89.
59. McCrindle, J.W., *IIAG.*; (Westminster, 1896), pp. 285, 296. For details about *Dvairājya* see also D.R. Bhandarkar's *Some Aspects of Ancient Hindu Polity* (Banaras, 1929), pp. 99-100.
60. *Av. Sam.*, 1, 21; 7, 45; 7, 85, 1; 7, 86, 1; 7, 117, 1; 2, 26; 11, 4; 19, 1, 15; *Ait. Br.*, 39, 2-4; *Tai. Sam.*, 2, 7, 15-17; *Bau. Gr. Sū.*, 1, 23; *Yāj. Saṁ.*, 1, 309 (Balabhatta, A.D. 1730-1820, in his

commentary on *Mitākṣara*, a comm. on this *Smṛti*, has discussed in detail); *Mbh. Śānti Parva*, 40, 9-15; also Ch. 39; *Av. Sam.*, 17, 1-10; 17, 11-34; *Viṣ. Dh. Pu.*, 2, 18, 2-4; *Rāj. Pr.*, pp. 42-43, 44-112; *Agn.*, 218, 2-35.

61. *Mbh. Ādi Parva* (Pāradi, 1968), 40, 6-7.
62. *Arth.*, III, 4, 2.
63. *Ep. Ind.*, VIII, pp. 36, 42 ff; also *Ep. Ind.*, IV, p. 2.
64. *Rājat.* (tr. by Aurel Stein, 2nd edn. Delhi, 1960 and R.S. Pandit, 1st edn. Allahabad, 1935, Delhi, 1968), V, 461-63.
65. *Ibid.*, 1, 325.
66. *Ibid.*, VII, pp. 773 ff.
67. Majumdar, R.C., *Corporate Life in Ancient India* (Calcutta, 1922), pp. 107-13.
68. *Ṛg. Saṁ.*, 1, 5, 6; 3, 50, 3; *Tai. Sam.*, 5, 2, 7.
69. *Ait. Br.*, III, 12, 19, 4; *Sat. Br.*, VII, 5, 3, 1-13.
70. *Arth.*, 1, 17. See also *Manu.*, 9, 201; *Śuk. Nīti.*, 1, 343-44; 1, 346-348; *Śānti Parva*, 31, 43; *Vana Parva*, 202, 8; *Vy.*, 88, 32.
71. *Śat. Br.*, 12, 9, 3, 1 & 3.
72. *JBORS*, Vol. III, p. 41.
73. *Śuk. Nīti.*, 1, 345.
74. *Śānti Parva*, 34, 31-33.
75. *Jāt.* Vol. I, p. 470; Vol. V, pp. 187 f; also Vol. I, p. 399.
76. *MAIMA*, (London, 1877), p. 200.
77. *Raghu.*, 29, 55 & 57.
78. *Ind. Ant.*, Vol. XXI, p. 156.
79. *Manu.*, VII, 2.
80. *Ibid.*, XII, 100.
81. *Hv.*, 3, 2, 35.
82. For details see *Mbh. Śānti Parva*, 57, 4-5, 11-19, 30-39; 108, 2-3 (for 36 qualities of a king); *Agn.* 238, 4-5; 239, 2-5, 6-10, 43-45; 223, 9-12 (for 21 qualities); *Manu.*, VII, 16-17, 19, 31-44 and 48; IX, 298-300; *Arth.*, VI, 1; VIII, 1; *Yāj. Sm.*, 1, 309-13; 330-36; *Gau. Dh. Sū.*, 11, 2-6; *Viṣ. Dh. Sū.*, 3, 1-20; *Viṣ. Dh. Pu.*, 2.3; *Kām. Nīti.*, 1, 21-22, 4, 6-24; 15, 31 (for 19 qualities); *Śuk. Nīti.*, 1, 73-86; *Mānaso.*, 2, 1, 1-9; 2, 1, 2-7 (for 44 qualities); *San. Sm.*; *Rājadharmakāṇḍa*, Ch. 3 (for 45 qualities); also *San. Sm.* (Bareli, 1980), 1.4; *Abhilāsi.*, 1.2.1;

1.2, 2-8 (for 44 qualities); see also *RNM.*, pp. 47-48; *Rāj. Pr.*, pp. 115-21; *NVA.* (by a Jain author Somadeva Suri, ed. Pannalal Soni, Bombay, V.E. 1979), 5, 55; 17, 33 ff; P.V. Kane, *History of Dharmaśāstra* (Hindi tr. by Arjun Chaube Kāsyapa, Lucknow, 1982), Vol. 2, pp. 597.

83. *Rāj. Pr.*, p. 30 (based on the Statement of Kātyāyana).
84. *Jāt.*, Vol. VIII, p. 111.
85. *Mbh. Śānti Parva*, 58, 1, also 2-20.
86. *Ibid.*, 68, 1-2, 8, 13-38, 39-53.
87. *Mats. Ch.*, 215, *VV.* 1-56; Ch. 220, *VV.* 1-46; *Agn.*, Ch. 223, *VV.*, 7-12.
88. *Manu.*, VII, 144.
89. *Arth.*, 1.19.
90. *Raghu.*, 14, 67.
91. For details see *Gau. Dh. Sū.*, 10, 7-8; 11, 9-10; 18, 31; *Vas. Dh. Sū.*, 19, 1.2, 7-8, *Viṣ. Dh. Sū.*, 3, 2-3, 79-80; *Yāj. Sm.*, 1, 335, also 315 and 323. See also *Dharmaśāstra Saṅgraha* ed. by Jivānanda Vidyāsāgara (Calcutta, 1876), Pt., I, pp. 60 ff; Pt. II, pp. 456 ff; *Smṛti Saṅgraha*, (Ānandāsrama edn. Poona, 1905); M.N. Dutta on *Vas.* and *Viṣ. Dh. Sū.* (Calcutta, 1908-9); *Śuk. Nīti.*, 1,14; 4, 7, 303; *Viṣ. Dh. Pu.* 3, 323, 25-26; *Śuk. Nīti.*, 1, 292, 311-13; *Manu.*, VII, 13 (Medhātithi, 805-900 A.D., the commentator of Manu also holds the same view); *Āp. Dh. Sū.*, 2, 10, 26, 2-3; *Rāj. Pr.*, pp. 254-55.
92. *Arth.*, VI, 1.
93. *Manu.*, VII, 69.
94. *Ibid.*, VIII, 258 and 262.
95. *Ibid.*, IX, 310.
96. *Ibid.*, IX, 272.
97. *Śuk. Nīti.*, 1, 183-87.

3

THE MINISTERS (Amātyas)

NEXT in importance to the king were the ministers, also known as *amātyas, mantrins* and *sacivas*. However, the connotation of these terms does not seem to be uniform.[1] Whatever may be their identifications and designations, it is a well proven fact that they constituted a very vital organ of the body politic. Besides, there were some other administrative officials who had to assist the king in the discharge of his daily duties.

The importance of ministers as counsellors or advisers, helpers, colleagues, guides, etc. to the king has been widely acknowledged by the political thinkers of ancient India. In the *Mahābhārata*[2] as well as the *Purāṇa*[3] it has been clearly stated that the king without ministers can neither defend the state nor can he run its administration. Therefore, it is the primary duty of the king to appoint ministers, who constitute the backbone of the state. It has been further pointed out that those states, whose kings after according proper honour to the ministers appoint them for the purpose of seeking their advice in matters of war and defence, prosper and thrive.[4] In the past every king was guided by his ministers.[5] Kauṭilya says that the state affairs cannot be conducted by the king without the assistance of competent councillors in the same manner as the carriage with one wheel cannot move. Thus the king should employ *amātyas* or ministers and hear their advice.[6] Manu has also pointed out that the king alone cannot shoulder the responsibilities of running the administration of state and hence he should appoint such ministers who are found gifted with all necessary qualities.[7] The assistants employed by king were called "*Sāhayāh*",[8] who shared the burden of the king in protecting his subjects.[9] One of them was the prime-minister, called "*amātyamukhya*", who was appointed to look after the people. He was supposed to be noble, learned and well-versed in *Dharmaśāstra*.[10] Yājñavalkya,[11] Vasiṣṭha,[12] Bṛhaspati,[13] Kātyāyana[14] and Śukra[15] have also highlighted the importance of the advice of ministers for the success of king as well as for the growth of the state.

A good deal of light has been thrown on the virtues of ministers, which they were supposed to be endowed with for managing the affairs of the state. Those, who were found wise, brave, diplomat, enthusiastic, efficient, honest, tolerant, farsighted and loyal and faithful to the king and the state, were appointed as ministers. They were also supposed to enjoy the confidence of the *Paura-Janapada*. One of their essential virtues was to maintain secrecy about war and politics and internal affairs of the state. It was also expected of them to be worthy of offering secret advise to the king.[16]

There seems to be divergence of opinion among different *ācāryas* about the mode of selection of *amātyas* as quoted by Kauṭilya. Ācārya Bhārdvāja holds that the king should appoint his colleagues as *amātyas*, because they are more faithful than others. But, on the other hand, Visālākṣa suggests that the persons extending co-operation to the king in managing the affairs of purely secret nature can be more suitable than the former as *amātyas*. But this is further contradicted by Parāṣara who thinks that only those, who can save the king from falling prey to any crisis or danger, can be made *amātyas*. Ācārya Piśuṇa (Nārada) thinks that it is devotion of the *amātyas* to the king and not a test of their political wisdom which is the supreme virtue. Therefore, according to him only those who prove their worth and ability while discharging the duties and responsibilities assigned to them can be appointed as *amātyas*. But Kauṇapadanta (Bhiṣma) does not give his assent to this view. He has pleaded that the position of *amātyas* should be offered merely on the hereditary ground. In support of his view he puts forth that such *amātyas* being well conversant with the customs and traditions of the past and closely connected with the king cannot betray him. Ācārya Vātavyādhi (Uddhava) does not support this view. He holds that the king knowing the science of polity should appoint others (who are quite new to him) as *amātyas*. But Bāhudantiputra (Indra) does not uphold it. He opines that the *amātyas* should not only be well versed in *Nītiśāstra*, but also practical realist, wise and faithful to the king. Kauṭilya, while attaching considerable importance to the views of *ācāryas* concerned, concludes that the king should not ignore even his colleagues. The king must appoint *amātyas* after taking into consideration their knowledge, wisdom, courage, virtues and vices, etc., but, he should not make them his ministers.[17] The *ācāryas* concerned were '*rājaśāstrapraṇetārah*,' who propounded theories before Kauṭilya as his precursors.

While showing the relative importance of all the seven organs of the state, different *ācāryas* have expressed different views. According to Bhārdwāja, the *amātyas* occupy more important position than the king. The safety of the state, collection of army, suppression of hostile forces, maintenance of income and expenditure, protection of princes and their coronation, etc. entirely depend on them. There can be no state administration without them. If they deviate from the right path or in case they let themselves down (called '*Vyasaṇa*'), state can face the problem. Their *Vyasaṇa* is more dangerous than that of the king, so far as the *Saptāṅga* state is concerned. The failure on their part to make arrangement for treaty and to repulse the constant attacks of the enemies were two different *Vyasaṇa*, called '*anaya*' and '*apanaya*' respectively. The *amātyas* have been called the heart and soul of the king. Therefore, they should be free from those vices or *Vyasaṇa*, which are detrimental to the interest of a king. But Kauṭilya holds different views. He says that the *amātyas* with vices can be easily replaced by those who are destitute of those vices. The king being the chief among all the seven organs of the state can make them virtuous. He can also remove the difficulties faced by the *amātyas, mantrins, purohitas, janapadas*, etc. and suggest improvement in their functioning styles. He, however, admits that everything depends on *amātyas*. All the works relating to the agriculture and forts, king and the state, establishment of the colonies and their progress, punishment of the culprits, collection of state taxes, the growth of *Janapada*, etc. are performed by the *amātyas*.[18]

Kauṭilya has divided the mantrins into three categories according to their qualities. Those who were of indigenous origin, noble family, firm determination and retentive memory, and artists, economists, wise, clever, orator, powerful, debator, enthusiastic, impressive, charming, tolerant, loyal to the king, gentle, capable, healthy, steadfast, etc. were considered worthy of being the prime minister.Those, who possessed either one fourth or half of these qualities were taken as ministers of middle or lower grade. The talents, loyalty, integrity and credibility of both the ministers and *amātyas* were tested, but methods employed were different. The king used to test the former by himself as well as through his colleagues and neighbours. Whereas, on the other hand, the king employed various secret means with the help of his *mantrins* and *purohitas* to test the conduct of the latter after being appointed. They had to undergo different kinds of tēsts. Those who passed the test in *Dharma* or law, were appointed to look after *Dharmasthāniya* (Civil Court) and *Kantakaśodhana* (Criminal Court). Those who passed the test in Economics, were appointed as *Samāhartā* (tax-collector) and *Sannidhāta* (treasurer). Those who were tested in the affairs of *Kāma* (sex-matter) were placed at *Vihāras* (place for enjoyment) and at *harem*. Those who were found fearless were appointed as body-guard of the king. It is really remarkable to note that only those *amātyas* who passed all these tests were appointed as ministers. And those who failed in all the tests were made incharge of different mines, forests and elephant force, etc.[19]

From the description provided by Kauṭilya it is quite evident that the *amātyas* and *mantrins* were the two different offices. The *amātyas*, of course, formed the part of *Mantri-pariṣada*, but all of them did not enjoy the rank of ministers. They were appointed for different positions. Only those who were found successful in all the tests conducted secretly to test their ability and loyalty were appointed as ministers. Whereas, on the other hand, the *manrins* were the members of the council of ministers as well as the advisers of the king. The rank and position of *mantrins* were higher than that of the *amātyas*.

Kauṭilya's statement regarding the test of *mantrins* can also be confirmed by the *Purāṇic* evidence[20] as well as by the statement of Manu.[21] The appointment of ministers at different places including gold and salt mines, market places, forests with elephants, etc. have also been referred to in the *Mahābhārata*[22] and *Manu Smṛti*.[23] It has been suggested that the Ministers should be selected only from amongst the *Brāhmaṇs*, *Kṣatriyas* and *Vaiśyas*, but not the *Śūdras*.[24] But, on the other hand, there is also a contradictory evidence to prove the inclusion of *Śūdras* in the ministry, as we shall see later.

The *mantri-parishad* or council of ministers was a very powerful body. The numerical strength of the ministry appears to have varied from time to time. There was no fixed number of ministers. The statements of both Manu[25] and Kauṭilya[26] prove that the number of ministers was determined according to the discretion of the king, the prevailing situation in the state and the necessity arising out of it, etc. The *Mahābhārata* categorically states that the minimum number of ministers should be three.[27] Further, in the same text it has been added that the king should make policy decision with the help of eight ministers,[28] out of which four should be *Brāhmaṇs*, three *Śūdras* and one *Suta* (or charioter).[29] The *Purāṇa* refers to seven officials appointed by the king.[30] The followers of Mānava, Bṛhaspati and Auśanasa schools were in favour of twelve *amātyas* and sixteen to twenty ministers respectively, as quoted by Kauṭilya himself.[31] Kāmandaka also refers to twelve *amātyas* in the council of ministers.[32] Manu[33] and Someśvara (1127-1138 A.D.)[34] were in favour of a smaller body consisting of either seven or eight ministers. Śukra has provided a list of eight to ten ministers.[35] The *Nītivākyāmṛita* has fixed the number of ministers from three to seven. In general cases the smaller body was preferred to a larger one. We have certain instances to show that a small state was managed with the help of four or five ministers. One of such instances was the "kingdom of the Silāhāras".[36] Anantadeva, the Silāhāra ruler, had a small ministry of only three in 1094 A.D. The state of Buddhist period had also four to five members in the council.[37]

The ministers had different designations, different portfolios and different functions.

According to Śukra, the following ten constituted the council of ministers : (1) *'Sumantra'*, or the Minister of Finance or Treasurer (equivalent to the *Vedic* term *Saṁgrahita* and Kauṭilya's *Samāhartā*), (2)

'Paṇḍita' or the Minister of Law or *dharma* and morality (similar to the *dharmamahāmātras* of Aśoka, the *śramanamahāmātras* under the Sātvāhanas, the *Vinayasthitiṣthāpakas* under the Guptas and *dharmāṅkuśas* under the Rāshṭrakūṭas), (3) *'Mantrin'* or incharge of both Foreign Ministry and Home Ministry (the epigraphic records designate them as *mahāsandhivigrahika*=officer incharge of peace and war), (4) *'Pradhāna'* or the premier, president of the council or the chief of the whole administration, (5) *'Sachiva'* or the War Minister (known as *Senāpati* under the Mauryas, *Mahābalādhikrita* under the Guptas and *Mahāprachanda-daṇḍanāyaka* under the Yādavas), (6) *'Amātya'* or the Revenue Minister, (7) *'prādvivāka'* or the Minister of Justice and *Nyāyādhisa* (Chief Justice), (8) *'Pratinidhi'* or Representative corresponding to the *Uparājā* of the *Jātakas*. (9) *'Purohita'* or the Minister of Religion (the Royal Chaplain of the *Vedic* period, *Purohita* of the epic age and *Sabhātthaka* of the *Jātakas* or Minister plenipotentiary. They ceased to be members of ministry from *c.* 200 A.D. onwards) and (10) *Duta* or Minister of Diplomacy.[38]

The number and designations of ministers and various other officials (appointed to assist the king in running the administration of the state) of the *Mantri-Parishad*, actually, varied from age to age. The *Mahābhārata* refers to members of the *Sabhā* (*Sabhāsadas*) designated as *Sahāyas* (the Ministers, *Amātyas*, or colleagues), *Sabhāyas* (or the Ministers with portfolios) and the *paricchada amātyas* (who were of native origin, learned, wise and loyal to the state).[39] The seven officials as referred to in the *Purāṇa* also included the spies, who had to travel in the disguise of a saint to collect information for the sake of the safety of the state.[40]

Manu refers to the Prime Minister (*Amātya-mukhya*),[41] finance officer enjoying the status of *amātyas*,[42] *Duta* (*rājaduta*) or the Minister of Diplomacy and *Senāpati*.[43] He has made it crystal clear that the king was incharge of both the state and the treasury; *Duta* had to deal with peace and war and the *Senāpati* had to command the different wings of the army.[44] The other officers of the executive were *Yukta* (VIII, 34) and *Mahāmātra* (IX, 259).

In the *Pāli* canon, the Prime Minister of *Ajātaśatru* has been called *Agra-mahāmātra* (the foremost minister). In the Aśokan inscriptions the high officials have been called *Mahāmātras* and *Dharma-Mahāmātrās* and other officials as *Rājukas*, *Yuktas* and *Prādeśikas*. In the *Divyāvadāna* the Chief Minister of Aśoka (Rādhā Gupta) is styled as *Amātya*.

Kauṭilya has provided the following list of 18 different officials who were incharge of different departments : (1) *Mantrin* (i.e. Adviser), who occupied supreme position among the Ministers, (2) *Purohita*, (3) *Senāpati* (the Minister incharge of the Army), (4) *Yuvarāja* or a prince holding the rank of the Minister, (5) *Dauvārika* or the Chief Officer functioning as a door-keeper of the palace, (6) *Antarvaṁśika* or the chief officer to look after the domestic affairs, (7) *Praśāstri* (*Praśāsta* or the Minister incharge of prison), (8) *Samāharta* or the Minister of Revenue, (9) *Saṇṇidhātri* or the Minister of Treasury, (10) *Pradeṣṭa* or incharge of issuing royal proclamation, (11) *Nāyaka* or the Chief army officer, (12) *Paura* or the Chief administrator of Capital cities, (13) *Vyāvahārika* or the judge or the Chief Justice, (14) *Kārmāntika* or the officer-in-charge of the mines and the factories, (15) *Mantri-Parishada-adhyaksha* or the president of the Council, (16) *Daṇḍa-pāla* or the Minister incharge of the maintenance of the Army, (17) *Durga-pāla* or the Minister incharge of *durgas* or forts or officer incharge of defending the state against the enemies and (18) *Antapāla* or Minister incharge of Frontiers.[45] The *Rājaduta* also found place in the Council of Ministers.[46] The protection of state also depended on the activities of the spies or officers engaged in the espionage department.[47]

The *Purohitas, Senāpati, Yuvarāj* and *Duta* used to play very important part in the protection of the king as well as the state. The *Purohitas* have been called the "defender and helper of the king and the *rāṣṭra* or state".[48] The *Brāhmaṇ* or *Purohita* also formed the part of *Mantri-Parishad* and their advice was also given due importance by the king.[49] The *Yuvarāja* or princes like other ministers were also the colleague of the king. Kauṭilya has fully discussed about them.[50] From the *Divyāvadāna* it appears that Aśoka's grandson Samprati was the *yuvarāja*. The *senāpati* used to advise the king about the strategy of war. The *Dutas* were of various kinds and had to perform various functions. But mainly they had to supply the king with all secret information, so as to enable him to take the step accordingly for the protection of his state.

One of the primary functions of the ministers was to give secret advice to the king. A very high importance has been attached to this aspect of the subject concerned. The good as well as the secret advice of the ministers not only constituted the basic foundation of the *rāṣṭra* or state of the king, but also paved the way for its growth. It was the duty of the king as well as his ministers to maintain secrecy about the planning, programme and contemplated action, war and peace, etc., which were decided by them through mutual consultations. The advice was like an armour for the king. It was the essence of the state-craft.[51] A great emphasis has been laid on the necessity of taking the secret advice by the king from his ministers separately.[52] But, on the other hand, we also find that the king used to consult his ministers separately as well as jointly. In this respect the statements of Kauṭilya[53] and Manu[54] go in harmony with each other. Kauṭilya has further made it clear that the king in order to maintain secrecy should not consult more than three or four ministers at a time. If necessary, he should decide the matter alone or with the consultations of one or two ministers. The advice centred round various subjects.[55] Manu has also stated that the king used to hold secret consultations with his ministers in the assembly hall or *Sabhā* after the dispersion of the common people therefrom.[56]

It was one of the main concerns of the ministers to keep an eye on the activities of enemies and to adopt every means to weaken them. If the king finds his enemy more stronger than him, he should enter into a treaty with him after consulting his ministers.[57] The ministers also used to supervise the works of other members of the council (*sabhāsadas* or councillors). In *nagaras* also officers were appointed to look after the general works.[58]

Śukra, one of the chief exponents of the *Saptāṅga*

theory of the state, has also laid stress on the fact that the king should never decide the policy matter alone. He must follow the advice of *Sabhāsadas* or the members of the advisory council like *Sabhya* (the president of the Council or *Mantri-Parishad*), *Adhikārins* (Ministers with portfolios or the heads of *Adhikaraṇas*, i.e. Departments) and the *Prakṛtis* (people's representatives dealing with various subjects). He further adds that the independent or unilateral decision of the king may prove ruinous for him. He may lose his state as well as the subjects.[59]

The evidence furnished by Manu shows that the king used to consult the ministers relating to the following six subjects : (1) Peace and War (*Saṁdhi-vigraha*), (2) *Sthāna* (state, capital cities, army and treasury), (3) source of income (*Samudaya*), (4) defence (*Gupti*), (5) preservation of wealth and (6) its equitable distribution.[60] There are also some other evidences to show that the ministers used to advise the king about the execution of the policy decision, protection of the king and the state, general administration, suppression of enemies, acquisition of territories and their defence, income and expenditure, measures to solve the problem arising out of the natural calamities, acquisition of wealth, the well being of the subjects, etc.[61] Both Manu[62] and Yājñavalkya[63] have stated that it was obligatory on the part of the king to consult the wisest and the most learned *Brāhmaṇ* (or *Purohita* holding the senior position among the ministers) on six various aspects of the polity immediately after consulting his ministers and before implementing any decision. The observation made by Manu in this regard is really very interesting.

He says that as tortoise takes his organs (feet and the mouth) inside, likewise the king should maintain secrecy about different organs (himself, *amātyas, rāṣṭra*, forts, treasury, army and friends). He should not let his enemies know about the secrets. Hence he should make constant efforts to know their secrets.[64]

Historical records bear an eloquent testimony to the importance of roles played by different ministers of different periods bearing different designations in running the administration of ancient Indian states as advisers of the king. Ajātaśatru of Magadha and king Prasenajit of Kosala were also dependent on the advice of their respective ministers. The *Jātakas* also refer to various ministers of the Buddhist period. Rock Edicts III and VI of Aśoka record that the council of ministers was a very useful political body during the period concerned. The literature as well as the inscriptions throw light on the functioning of the *Mantri-Parishad* under the Mauryas, the Śungas, the Guptas, the Maukharis, the Paramāras, the Rashtrakutās, the Chālukyas and the Śilāhāras of the Deccan, the rulers of Kashmir and various other rulers of different ancient dynasties.

NOTES AND REFERENCES

1. The earliest references to mantrins (*amāvān*) and *amātya* occur in the *Ṛg. Sam.*, 4.4.1 and 7.15.3 respectively; see also *Nirukta* 6.12. The *amātya* has been used in the sense of *mantrin* for the first time in *Āp. Dh. Sū.*, 2.10.25.10. In *Ait. Br.* the word *Saciva* figures. In *Vāl. Rām.* (*Bālakāṇḍa*, text with Hindi tr. by Yudhiṣṭhira Mīmāṁsak and ed. by Pt. Akhilanand, Amritasar, V.E. 2025, 7, 1-4; 8, 4) *amātya* has been distinguished from *mantrin*, but in *Yuddha Kāṇḍa* (text

with Hindi tr. by Pt. Vijayapāla, Bahalgaḍh, V.E. 2029, 130, 18 and 21) *mantrins* and *sacivas* have been used separately, however, both seem to be identical. Kauṭilya (*Arth.*, 1.7 and 8) has differentiated between *amātyas* and *mantrins*. Kāmandaka (*Kām. Nīti.*, 4, 25, 27; 13, 24, 64) has used *saciva* and *amātya* in an identical manner. In *Rājanītiprakāśa* (p. 178) *amātyas* have been identified with *mantrins*. *Amk.* (2, 8.4), while making a clear distinction between the various terms used for *mantrins*, states that the *amātyas* designated as '*dhīsaciva*' and *mantrin* were different from '*karmasaciva*', who were the *mantrin* for giving advice to the king on all spheres of activities. These are the minor or nominal differences between the various terms used for ministers, which hardly matter.

2. *Mbh. Śānti Parva*, 116, 12-14.
3. *Mats.*, 215, 2-3.
4. *Mbh. Śānti Parva*, 92, 28.
5. *Ibid.*, 69, 22.
6. *Artha.*, 1.3.7.
7. *Manu.*, VII, 55.
8. *Manu.*, VII, 31.
9. *Ibid.*, VII, 36.
10. *Ibid.*, VII, 141.
11. *Yāj. Sm.*, 1. 311-12.
12. *Vaṣ. Sm.*, 325-331.
13. *Bṛh. Sm.*, 1, 4-5.
14. *cf.* Viramitrodaya, p. 14.
15. *Śuk. Nīti.*, 2, 1-7. Se also *Rāj. Pr.*, p. 174; *Viṣ. Dh. Pu.*, 2, 24, 2-3.
16. *Mbh. Śānti Parva*, 84, 22, 24, 28-32, 43-50; 86, 7-31; 116, 15-17; 118, 2-3 (where 14 qualities of ministers have been focussed); *Āshramavāsika Parva*, 9, 14; *Mats.*, 215, 2.7; *Agn.*, 239, 11-23; *Manu.*, VII, 54, 60-62; *Yāj. Sm.*, 1, 312; *Kām. Nīti.*, 4, 25-30; Candeśvara's *RNR.* (ed. by K.P. Jayaswal, Bihar and Orissa Research Society, 1924), pp. 13-14; *Rāj. Pr.*, pp. 174-178; *Rājadharmakaustubha* (of Anantadeva, 1650-1680), pp. 251-54, *cf.* P.V. Kane, *op. cit.*, pp. 624-25.

17. *Arth.*, 1.3.7.
18. *Ibid.*, VIII, 1.
19. For details see *Ibid.*, 1.4.8; 1.5.9.
20. *Agn.*, 239, 17-23.
21. *Manu.*, VII, 54 and 60.
22. *Mbh. Śānti Parva*, 69, 28.
23. VII, 62.
24. *Mbh.* (*Āshramavāsika Parva*, 9.20); *Agn.* (239, 15-16); *Manu.* (VII, 58) and Kauṭilya (*Arth.* 1, 4, 8) refer to *Brāhmaṇs* or *Purohitas*. But *Śuk. Nīti.* (2, 426-27) and *Nītivākyāmṛta* (p. 108, *cf.* P.V. Kane, *op. cit.*, p. 625) refer to the *Brāhmaṇs, Kṣatriyas* and *Vaiśyas* as ministers.
25. *Manu.* VII, 61.
26. *Arth.* 1.15.
27. *Mbh. Śānti Parva*, 84, 44.
28. *Ibid.*, 86, 10.
29. *Ibid.*, 86, 7-9. In the interpolated versions of the text of different other recensions number varies from 32 to 37 comprising the 4 *Brāhmaṇs*, 8 *Kṣatriyas*, 21 *Vaiśyas* and 3 to 6 *Śūdras*. We do not have any evidence to confirm this inflated number.
30. *Mats.*, 215, 43, see also 215, *Vv.* 22-42.
31. *Arth.* 1.15.
32. *Kām. Nīti.*, 1. 167-68.
33. *Manu.*, VII, 54.
34. *Mānaso.*, 2, 2.57.
35. *Śuk. Nīti.*, 2, 71-72, 84-87.
36. *Ind. Ant.*, Vol. V, p. 278; Vol. IX, p. 35.
37. *Jāt.* no. 528.
38. For details see *Śuk. Nīti.*, 2, 70-72, 84-87, 89, 95-101.
39. *Mbḥ. Śānti Parva*, 83, 1-4.
40. *Mats.*, 215, 22-43, 90-99.
41. *Manu.*, VII, 141..
42. *Manu.*, VII, 60.
43. *Manu.*, VII, 64-67 and 153.
44. *Manu.*, VII, 65
45. *Arth.*, 1.12.

46. *Ibid.*, 1.16.
47. *Ibid.*, 1, 11-12.
48. *Ait. Br.*, 40.2; *Śuk. Nīti.*, 2, 74. See also *Viṣ. Dh. Sū.*, 3, 70; *Yāj. Sm.*, 1, 313 and *Kām. Nīti.*, 4, 32 for the importance of *Purohitas*.
49. *Yāj. Sam.*, 1, 312-13; *Arth.*, 1.8-9.
50. *Arth.*, 1.17.
51. For details see *Mbh. Śānti Parva*, 84, 45-50; *Mats.*, 220, 31-36; *Agn.*, 239, 15-16; *Yāj. Sm.*, 1, 344. *Vaṣ. Sm.*, 325-27; *Kām. Nīti.*, 11, 53, 65-66; 13, 23-24; *Mānaso.*, 2.9; *Manu.*, VII, 147.
52. *Mbh. Āshramavāsika Parva*, 9, 21, 24-25; *Mats.*, 215, 48-49; 220, 38-40.
53. *Arth.*, 1.15.
54. *Manu.*, VII, 57.
55. *Arth.*, 1.15.
56. *Manu.*, VII, 146. See also VII, 55, 58-59, 104.
57. *Mbh. Śānti Parva*, 69, 14; 84, 45.
58. *Ibid.*, 88, 10.
59. *Śuk. Nīti.*, 2, 2-4.
60. *Manu.*, VII, 56. See also V.S. Agrawala, *India as Described by Manu.* (Varanasi, 1970), p. 49.
61. *Arth.*, 1.15; *Agn.*, 241, 4, 16-18; *Kām. Nīti.*, 10, 56; 13, 23-24; *Mānaso.*, 2, 9, 697.
62. *Manu.*, VII, 58-59.
63. *Yāj. Sm.*, 1. 312.
64. *Manu.*, VII, 105.

4

THE TERRITORY AND THE PEOPLE (Janapada / Rāṣṭra)

THE *janapada or rāṣṭra* (territorial units) falls in order as third important organ of the state after the king and the Ministers.[1] It has rightly been called as "*rājya-bhumi*", [2] which literally means the territory of the state. Since it has been described in different literary texts as one of the seven constituents of state, its identification with the Indian Nation or the country, as a whole, will not be justified at all.

The word *'rāṣṭra'* figures in the *Vedic* literature[3] as the state of the king, as a territory, *deśa* (country denoting a particular region) and *pradeśa* (*janapada*) with little variations in context of their meanings and explanations as given therein. The progress and prosperity of the state was the ultimate goal of the king in the *Vedic* age too. The *Vedic* concept of *rāṣṭra,* however, does not differ much from that of the post-*Vedic* one.

Vālmīki had also very distinct conception of *Janapada* or *rāṣṭra*. He has used *Janapada, rāṣṭra* and *deśa* interchangeably for state and its territories and put emphasis on the fact that *Janapada* or *rāṣṭra* without king leads to anarchy, chaos and confusion.[4] The reference to a *Kausala deśa* surrounded by an extensive *rāṣṭra*[5] fairly illustrates the truth that the word *rāṣṭra* denotes nothing other than the territorial units of the state in the present context. The people inhabiting a *Janapada* has been collectively called '*Jānapadāh*', '*Janapada-nivāsi*' or '*Janapadavāsi*' and those inhabiting *Pura* (*nagara* or capital city) as *pura-vāsi*, and both were jointly known as "*Paura-Jānpadah*".[6]

Vyāsa had distinguished *rāṣṭra*[7] from *Janapada*.[8] The former is the substitute of *rājya* or state and the latter stands for its different territorial units. The people inhabiting the *rāṣṭra* have been described in the *Mahābhārata* as *rāṣṭravāsi* or *rājyavāsi*. The growth of the state depended on mutual co-operation of its king and his subjects living in different Janapadaṣ and Puras.

The *Purāṇas* refer to both *Janapada* and *rāṣṭra* (having the same meaning) as the third organ of the state.[9] The *Janapada* of Yājñavalkya[10] and *rāṣṭra* of Viṣṇu[11] are identical in nature. The *rāṣṭra*[12] of Manu is one of the chief organs of the state; his *Janapada*[13] is territory and *Vishya* (*deśa*)[14] a part of *rāṣṭra*. The people of a *rāṣṭra* were called "*Raṣṭrikas*".[15] V.S. Agrawala, while interpreting the data supplied by Manu has observed that the "*Rāshtra*" was a kingdom. It was the "collective name of the king's sphere of administration. The *Rāshtra, Rājā* and *Prajā* were limbs of one body-politic . . . It comprised several countries . . . There were several units of administration. These were either called '*Vishaya*' or likely *Janapadas* (='*provinces*'). The word *Rāshtra* used in plural number also signifies parts of a kingdom."[16]

The epic does not make much difference between the *Janapada, Rāṣṭra, Vishaya* and *Deśa.*[17] All these terms have been used for the territory of a state as a whole, whereas some of the epigraphic records refer to them as different divisions of territory or state. As a matter of fact, these terms signify both the territory and the population. Land and the people denoting a *Janapada* or *rāṣṭra* constituted an essential element of the state. Both were equally important for the existence and growth of the state. That is why, it has been said that the land should be fertile, covered with forest and watered by rivers. There should be suitable places for establishing villages and cities and they should be provided with all means of communication. The people should also be industrious and followers of the *Dharma*.

The epic also enjoins the king to protect both land and the people from external aggressions. He should make all possible efforts to promote the economic prosperity of the state. The territory inhabited by worthy people and marching towards material prosperity helps to strengthen the position of the king. Such territory has been called "*Sphitajanapada*".[18] *Pañchāl, Chedi, Matsya, Śurasena, Pataccara Daśārna, Navarāṣṭra, Malla, Shālva* and *Yugandhara* were some of the prosperous *Janapadas* or states surrounding Kuru *Janapada* or *rājya.*[19] *Champāpuri* and *Aṅga* have been referred to as *rājya, deśa*, *nagara* and *vishaya,*[20] which are synonymous terms. Further, *nagara*, *rājya* and *rāṣṭra,*[21] on the one hand, and *pur* and *rāṣṭra* (*rājya*), on the other, have also been used together.[22]

If the logical interpretation of the term *Janapada* or *rāṣṭra,* which includes the rural areas as well as the territory of a state having both cities and villages alike, is accepted, U.N. Ghosal's[23] identification of *rāṣṭra* only with 'rural area' can be disproved of.

Manu also cites the examples of Kurukṣetra, Matsya (virāta), Pañchāla ("Kanyakubja and Ahicchetra) and Śurasena (Mathura) as territorial states.[24]

Kauṭilya's *Janapada* (which has been used in place of *rāṣṭra* as an organ of the state) comprised several villages and towns (*pura*).[25] He has, actually, divided the whole *rāṣṭra* into two parts i.e. *pura* and *janapada*. Actually, the *rāṣṭra* in a wider context included *pur* or *nagar*, *Janapada* and *nigama* or *naigama* (corporate association of guilds merchants). Yājñavalkya also refers to *Janapadas*, *gañas*, *śṛenis* and *jātis* (castes) as units following their own rules.[26]

In the Buddhist texts[27] *Jānapadāḥ* appear as inhabitants of the *Janapada*. The *Jātakas* and Pāli canon have *Janapada* and *nigama*, and Sanskrit texts have *Paura* and *Janapada*.

The Amarakośa does not make much distinction between the *rāṣṭra, janapada, deśa* and *visaya*. The *rāṣṭra* has been identified with territory and shown as one of the organs of the state. The *Janapada* (*Jānapadāḥ*) includes villages and towns. *Deśa* and *Visaya* (synonym) including groups of villages are described as parts of a *rāṣṭra*.[28] Thus, *Janapada, deśa* or *Visaya* seem to have formed the part of a *rāṣṭra*. Somadeva (ascribed to the post-tenth century, different from Somadeva of Kashmir, who composed his *Kathāsarit-sāgar* in the eleventh century) in his *Nītivākyāmṛta*[29] has also described the *rāṣṭra*, *Janapada, Visaya,* and *deśa* more or less in the same manner. Daṇḍin has also referred to the *Janapada* and *rāṣṭra* as synonymous.[30] *Aparārka* or *Aparāditya* (1100-1200 A.D.), while quoting Vyāsa (*smṛtikāra*) in his commentary on *Yājñavalkya Smṛti*, has also used *Janapda-deśa* together.[31] Mitra Mishra in the "*Vira-mitrodaya*"[32] has used "*Paura Janapada*" together as inhabitants of *Pura* and *Janapada.*

In the epigraphic records : (a) *Hāthīgumphā* cave inscription of king *Khāravela* (*c.* 170 B.C.)[33] and (b) Junagarh Rock inscription of Rudradāman I (*Śāka*, 72=A.D. 150)[34] "*Paura-Janapada*" have been used for the inhabitants of *Pura* or *Nagara* and *Janapada* respectively.

K.P. Jayaswal also takes *Janapada*, *rāṣṭra* and *deśa* as synonymous. He describes the term *Janapada* as "the seat of the nation." True, but "*Paura-Janapada*" were not the two corporate political bodies or institutions, as described by him. On the basis of the use of the terms "*Paura-Jānapada*" in the plural sense in the literature and inscriptions, he has called the former as Assembly of the Capital City and the latter as Assembly of the *Janapada* (600 B.C.-600 A.D.),[35] which is hardly convincing. Actually, the *Paura* were the people of the *Pur, Nagara* or Capital City and the *Jānapadāḥ* the people of villages and other urban areas far away from the capital. They may be having their own rulers, administrative set-up, law and constitution, but it does not mean that they represent political bodies. Any way, since this does not fall within the purview of the treatment of the subject concerned, it is better to refrain from going into further details and to concentrate upon the main subject.

Ācārya Viśālākṣa, Kauṭilya and Kāmandaka are more or less of the same view about the importance of *rāṣṭra* or *Janapada* as one of the organs of state.

According to Viśālākṣa, the *Janapada* is relatively more important organ of the state than *amātyas*. He further observes that the wealth, armed forces, clothes, various kinds of metals, etc. are all obtained from it. The misfortune befalling it is more dangerous than that of *amātyas*. Its fall leads to the destruction of king, *amātyas* and many other things. While adding something more to it, Kauṭilya says that the existence of forts, treasury and army absolutely depends on the *Janapada*. He considers *Janapada* more important than forts. He, however, does not deny that the existence of one depends on the other. He further makes it clear that for the creation of forts the *Janapada* is necessary and likewise for the protection of the latter the former is indispensable. The life of the people living in a *Janapada* without fort, according to him, is not safe.[36] Kāmandaka had gone to the extent of saying that all other organs of the state spring forth from the *rāṣṭra*, therefore, the king should make all possible efforts for its growth and development.[37]

In order to carve out or set up a *Janapada* or to create a *rāṣṭra* and to ensure its all round progress and prosperity the king used to select such a territory which, collectively speaking, was extensive, productive and surrounded by rivers, mountains, forests (including the forest of elephants) and beautiful gardens; whose climate was conducive for the good health of the citizens; where adequate facilities were available for growing maximum crops with minimum amount of labour; where domestication of animals was possible; there were grazing fields and agricultural facilities; means of livelihood were easily available;

there were land and sea routes, there were big mines, big markets, other trading centres for selling and purchasing and suitable places for import and export, which was inhabited by *Āryans, Vaiśyas, Śūdras,* artisans, craftsmen, traders and merchants and other lower class people; where people from different countries came, settled and maintained cosmopolitan outlook; which was dominated by those people who were basically opposed to the hostile king; whose neighbouring kings were very weak and *Sāmantas* were brought under control; in the middle of which as well as at its frontiers there were impregnable forts and whose farmers were industrious, the chiefs were learned and wise and the subjects were devoted and loyal to the king and able to bear the burden of taxes and the punishments imposed on them.[38]

The territory and population being the pre-requisite conditions for the creation of a *rāṣṭra* or state were always kept in view by ancient Indian kings. Kauṭilya has categorically stated that a king either by inviting the people from other countries (*deśa* or *rāṣṭra*) or by increasing the population of his own country should revive old *Janapada* or create a new one. Each *Janapada* should consist of villages with minimum 100 and maximum 500 houses and should be inhabited mostly by the *Śūdras* and farmers. The distance of one village from the other should not be more than either one or two *krosa* (2 or 4 miles), so that they may help each other in necessity. The boundary of a well-settled village should be fixed by planting trees or by rivers, mountains, forests, etc.[39]

The system of making land grants to the *Brāhmaṇs* for their territorial settlements also appears to have been in vogue. In this regard the information supplied by Yājñavalkya seems to be of great historical value. He says : "The king after having made land-grants to the *Brāhmaṇs* and settled the amount of tax to be paid by them should issue a copper-plate bearing an inscription containing the names of rulers of his dynasty and the details about the extent of land granted with boundary on all its four sides. He should also put his seal showing his name and order. While putting his signature and recording time and date thereon, he should also mention about the rules to be followed by the future rulers for maintaining that grant".[40] Kauṭilya puts it in somewhat different way. He says that the king must make land-grants to the *Brāhmaṇs*, including *Ācāryas*, *Purohitas, Shrotriyas* and others, but he should neither collect tax from them nor should he take the granted land back. He should also make land grants to his subjects and other officials and staffs comprising departmental heads (*adhyakṣas*), *Saṁkhyāyakas* (clerks), *Gopas* or village officers (or officer-in-charge of 10 villages each), *Sthānikas* (officer designate for looking after *Nagaras*), Physicians, *Janghākārikas* (earning living in farflung areas), *Anikasthas* (incharge of elephants) and others and should not allow them either to sell or mortgage that land.[41]

Steps were also taken to make suitable administrative arrangements for each unit of the *rāṣṭra* and for its defence. Administration was carried on through a hierarchy of officials appointed by the king for smaller as well as bigger areas.

The smallest unit of the administration was a village, which was ruled by a chief or headman called

"*Grāmādhīpati*" or "*Grāmādhyaksa*". The chief of the ten villages was known as "*Daśagrāmādhipati*" or "*Daśādhyakṣa*". *Above him was the chief of the twenty villages, who was, possibly, called Viṁsādhyakṣa.* Next in grade was the chief of a hundred villages, known as "*Śatagrāmādhipati*" or "*Śatādhyakṣa*". The sovereign ruling over a thousand villages was known as "*Rāṣṭriya*" His jurisdiction extended to vast areas corresponding to a district or a branch town (*kasvā*) and he fixed his headquarters in the *pura* or chief town of that district. The lord of whole "*Visaya*" was designated as "*Visayeśvara*" or "*Visayapati*". The chief ruler of *deśa* has been called "*Deśādhyakṣa*". The *deśa* or *Visaya* was, of course, a bigger unit. The ruler of whole *rāṣṭra* was perhaps called "*Rāstrapati*"[42] and, above all, the king was the head of the whole state by virtue of his being the "sole protector of people".

Each chief was responsible for maintaining law and order in the areas falling within their respective jurisdiction and spheres of their activities. One chief was supposed to report the matter to other, who happened to be more competent than him, and, of course, it was done from lower level to higher level. An excellent example has also been presented about the democratic way of functioning of all the chiefs and of their coordinated efforts to settle all the matters.

It has been said that the detailed information about the day-to-day affairs of the *Janapada*, law and order problem, disputes and any other occurrences was sent from the chief of a village to the chief of ten villages and from there to the chief of twenty villages, who was further responsible to inform everything to the chief of hundred villages and finally he had to pass on the same to the chief of a thousand villages or *Deśādhyakṣa*, and in this way they mutually co-operated with each other to settle the problems concerned of each *Janapada*.[43]

The income collected from villagers constituted the source of maintenance of each chief. The village headman was entitled to receive from the villagers what they used to give to the king, *i.e.* corn, fuel, etc. The ruler of ten villages enjoyed the right of free use of land equal to one "*Kullam*" (plot of land with fixed area), and the chief of twenty villages had in his possession the land equal to five "*Kulas*". The chief of a hundred villages was entitled to receive the revenues of one village, which was his headquarters controlled by many other subordinate officials appointed by him. The ruler (*'Rāṣṭriya'*) of a thousand villages, who was the most honourable for the people, was allowed by the king to receive the revenue of a *'pur'* or a *'Śākhā-Nagara'* or branch town (*Kasbā*), to take share of the produce and to enjoy all other things which were available there.[44]

According to Śukra, the chief of one hundred villages was called *Sāmanta* and other officials appointed for this particular unit were designated as *Anu-Sāmanta* and the headman of ten villages was known as *Nāyaka*.[45] Kauṭilya has referred to different administrative units which were set up in different parts of a *Janapada*. According to him also, the smallest unit of a *Janapada* was *Grāma*. A block consisting of ten villages was known as *'Saṁgrahaṇa'*, two hundred villages as "*Kharvatika*", four hundred villages as "*Dronamukha*" and eight hundred villages, as "*Sthāniya*".[46] These were the different names of headquarters. Manu has also stated that for the protection of a *rāṣṭra*, in the centre of each block consisting of two, three and five villages one officer appointed by the king was placed and for the management of a hundred villages one chief officer was appointed separately.[47]

Kauṭilya has further pointed out that it was the duty of *Samāhartā* to divide the whole *Janapada* into four parts, to put it into three categories, *i.e.* higher, middle and lower and to record their number, production, geographical situation, etc. into his register. He had also to record the details about the villages which were put into three categories, *i.e.* (a) villages not paying any tax, (b) villages from where armed forces were regularly recruited and (c) villages which paid taxes or tribute in the form of corns, animals, gold, silver, menial labour, etc. An administrative unit consisting of five to ten villages each was managed by an officer designated as *Gopas*. They had to work under the supervision of *Samāhartā*. They had to maintain the records of population structure of each village. The Register also contained the number of *Brāhmaṇs, Kṣatriyas, Vaiśyas, Śūdras*, farmers, traders, artisans, slaves, tax-payers, etc. living in villages. In each of the four *Janapadas* or *rāṣṭra* an officer designated as "*Sthānika*" was appointed who had also to do the same work. The *Gopas* and *Sthānikas* were assisted by *Pradeṣṭa* in running the administration of *rāṣṭra*.[48]

The king used to appoint a minister, who was his adviser and well-wisher, to supervise the works of the chiefs of villages.[49] The spies were also deputed in *Pur* as well as in different parts of *Janapada* to collect information about the functioning of different officials.[50] Different other officials and departmental heads were also appointed by the king to look after the works relating to political, religious and economic affairs.[51]

The age-long tradition of keeping different officials in the state to supervise different works are well recorded in literature and inscriptions. During the time of Aśoka *Mahāmātra, Yukta, Rajuka*, etc. were appointed. The epigraphic records[52] show that during the times of the Guptas the provincial rulers appointed by the emperors were called *Uparīka* and *Mahārāja* and the District administrators were known as *Visayapatis*. The copper plate of Kumaragupta I also refers to *"Gramāsta-Kulādhikarnama*, which shows that an administrative unit for eight villages was set up.

According to Kauṭilya, forts were erected at the frontiers of *Janapadas* under the guidance of *Antapāla* for providing security to *rāṣṭra*. Besides, some of the forest tribes like the *Śabaras*, *Pulindas* and *Cāṇḍālas* were assigned the duties of guarding the frontiers of *Janapadas*.[53] The defence of the *rāṣṭra* was a subject of utmost importance for the king not only for his own survival, but also for the well-being of his subjects and for the prosperity of the whole state.[54] It has been very beautifully said that the king, whose *Janapada* or *Pura* is rich and prosperous and well equipped with happy and contented subjects and faithful ministers, can be called *Prithvipati*.[55]

It has been said that the inhabitants of *rāṣṭra* for the sake of safety of their own life and property must have a strong king, otherwise it will lead to an anarchy.[56] If an *arājaka rāṣṭra* (a state where there is anarchy and despotism), whose king is very weak, worthless and incompetent, is attacked by a king, who is stronger, powerful and competent and desirous of ruling over a state, the subjects over there should come forward to welcome him and accept him as a king in the general interest of the state.[57]

The king was not only supposed to defend the territorial integrity of his own *rāṣṭra* (*Svarāṣṭra*), but also to watch the activities of the king of hostile *rāṣṭra* (*Śatru-rāṣṭra* or *Para-rāṣṭra*) lying adjacent to his territory. The network of espionage activities was extended to both.[58]

Thus, on the whole, we find that the settlements of population of various grades in both old and new *Janapadas* comprising several units proved to be very helpful factor in the state formation process. The progress of the state largely depended on the extension of its territory (*rāṣṭra*) and the setting up of different administrative units controlled by different officials.

NOTES AND REFERENCES

1. *Agn.*, 239, 2; also 225, 12; see also *Viṣ. Dh. Pu.*, 11.65.22.
2. *Ibid.*, 239, 24-25 (translated version).
3. *Ṛg. Sam.*, 4, 42, 1; 7, 34, 11; 7, 84, 2; 10, 109, 3; 10, 173, 1-6; 10, 174, 1; *Av. Sam.*, 12, 1, 8; *Yv.*, (*Vāj. Sam.*), 22, 22; *Tai. Br.*, 3, 8, 13; *Tai. Sam.*, 7, 5, 18.1.

   Rāṣṭra of the *Ṛgvedic Āryans* was also identical with *deśa* or *rājya*. The concept of *Svrājya* had already emerged in the *Ṛgvedic* India, and, therefore, for its stability and prosperity they used to invoke their gods. (See also Viśveśvaranath Reu, *Ṛgveda par ek itihāsika driṣṭi*, Delhi, 1967, pp. 209, 211). The territorial concept, of course, entered upon a new phase of orientation in the later *Vedic* period, which finds confirmation in 63 hymns of *Sūkta*—I of Ch. 12 (*'Bhumi Sukta'*) of *Av. Sam.* From this *Vedic* text it appears that for the formation and evolution of the state it was necessary that each territorial unit or *rāṣṭra*, whether small or big, should be treated like motherland on the emotional basis. However, the *Vedic* concept of *rāṣṭra* was not at all based on modern concept of nationalism. Each group wanted to have strong and stable *rāṣṭra*. (See also *Ācārya* Priyavrata Vedavācaspati, *Vedoṅ ke Rājanītika Siddhānta*, Meerut, 1983, pp. 15-21). The details alluding to the subject concerned have been furnished in the *Yv.* in a much more wider context than what we find in other *Saṁhitās*. That is why, V.S. Agrawala (*Itihāsa-Darśana—a collection of his papers*, ed. by P.K. Agrawala, Varanasi, 1978, pp. 101-2) has connected this particular description of *rāṣṭra* with *Bhārata Rāṣṭra*, which is not beyond dispute.

4. *Vāl. Rām., Ayodhya Kāṇḍa* (text ed. and tr. by Pt. Akhilānanda, Amritsar, V.E. 2019), 67, 8-38.
5. *Ibid.*, 49, 13.
6. *Ibid.*, 2, 19; 6, 25-26 and 28; 14, 55.
7. *Mbh.*, *Śānti Parva*, 57, 5; 59, 51; 69, 62-63; 60, 3; 67, 2-6.
8. *Ibid.*, 69, 10; 84, 43; 92, 22-23; 95, 3 and 5; *Āshramavāsika Parva*, 9, 26. See also V.S. Agrawala, *Bhā. Sāv.* (Delhi, 1968), vol. 3, pp. 41-58. One particular passage inserted in the *Bhiṣma Parva* (ed. with Hindi tr. by Damodar, Sātvalekar, Pāradi, 1972, 10, 5-9), is of exceptional value. It reflects the age-old tradition of showing the love for the country—Bharata—by its different rulers succeeding from Manu to the king Dilip and points to their feelings of partiotism or emotional attachment to the country. V.S. Agrawala ("*Bhārat-Vaṅdana*", *cf. Itihāsa-Darśana*, p. 100; "*Bhāratīya Jṅāna-Gaṅgā ke Bhagirath* : Maharshi Vedavyāsa", *cf. Viswa-Bhārati,* II, Lucknow, 1958, pp. 725-26) has called this as "*rāṣṭra-gita*" and in it he finds the reflection of the concept of *Bhārata-Rāṣṭra*. However, this is not directly related to the theory under discussion.
9. *Mats.*, 220, 19 (for *Janapada*); *Agn.*, 239, 1 (for *rāṣṭra*).
10. *Yāj. Sm.*, 1. 353 and 361.
11. *Viṣ. Sm.*, 3, 33.
12. *Manu.*, IX, 294.
13. *Ibid.*, VIII, 41.

14. *Ibid.* VII, 134.
15. *Ibid.*, X, 61.
16. *India as described by Manu*, pp. 46-47. See also his article "*Bhāratīya Samāja-Vyavasthā ke Pratishthāpak : Prajāpati Manu*", *Viswa-Bhārati* (for Manu and Rāṣṭra), 11. p. 757.
17. *Mbh.*, IV, (*Virāta Parva,* Pāradi, 1969), 1, 8-9; 6-9; III, (*Āraṇyaka Parva*, Pāradi, 1969), 36, 28; 113, 15; 129, 3.
18. *Mbh. Śānti Parva*, 95, 3-5.
19. *Mbh. Virāta Parva*, 1, 9.
20. *Mbh. Āraṇyaka Parva*, 113, 15.
21. *Mbh. Śānti Parva*, 89, 13, 14.
22. *Ibid.*, 308, 153-54.
23. Ghoṣal, U.N., *A History of Indian Political Ideas* (Oxford, 1959), p. 445.
24. *Manu.*, VII, 193.
25. *Arth.*, Bk. II, Chs. 1-3; VI, 1; VIII, 1.
26. *Yāj. Sm.*, 1, 360-61.
27. *Jāt.*, I, p. 149; *DN., Kūṭadanta Sutta*, Para-12.
28. *Amk.*, 2, 1.8, fn. 1-2; 2, 8.17; 3, 3, 184, fn. 2 and 3.
29. *Janapadasamuddeśa*, p. 19 quoted in P.V. Kane, *op. cit.*, p. 640.
30. *Dask., Ucch.*, 3.
31. *Yājñavalkya,* II, 92; See also *Aparārka-Yājñavalkya-Dharmaśāstra Nivandha*, Pub. in 2 Vols., Ānandāsrama edn. Poona; R. Shama Sastry in his tr. of *Arth.* (Bangalore, 1915, pp. 45-46, fn.) has also referred to "*Janapada-deśa*".
32. Mitra Mishra, *Viramitrodaya*, p. 11.
33. Sircar, D.C., (ed.) : *SI.* (Calcutta, 1965), Vol. 1, line 7, p. 215. See also Prinsep, *JASB.*, VI, pp. 1075-91. *Cor. Inc. Ind.*, 1, pp. 27 f, 98-101, 132 ff; K.P. Jayaswal, *JBORS.*, III, 1917, pp. 451, 456; K.P. Jayaswal and R.D. Banerji, *Ep. Ind.*, XX, pp. 71-72; Fleet, *JRAS.*, 1910, pp. 242 ff.
34. *SI.* Vol. I, Line 16, p. 180; also line 11, p. 178; See also *JBBRAS.*, VII, pp. 113 ff. For further discussion on *Rāṣṭra* and *Viṣaya* see *Ind. Ant.*, VIII, p. 20; XII, pp. 247 and 251 and *Ep. Ind.* I, p. 5; XIV, p. 121.
35. *Hindu Polity*, pp. 229-35 and 245-69; B.K. Sarkar (*Political Institutions and Theories of the Hindus*, Calcutta, 1939, pp.

71 f) and Beni Prasad (*The State in Ancient India*, Allahabad, 1928, pp. 498-500) have also criticised the *Paura-Janapada* theory as expounded by Mr. Jayaswal.

36. *Arth.*, VIII, 1.
37. *Kām. Nīti.*, 6, 3; See also *NVA.* p. 7.
38. *Arth.*, II, 1; VI, 1; *Manu.*, VII, 69; *Yāj. Sm.*, 1, 321; *Viṣ. Sm.*, 3, 4-5; *Agn.*, 239, 24-27; *Mats.*, 217, 1-5; *Viṣ. Dh. Pu.*, 2, 26, 1-5; *Mānaso.*, 2, 3, 151-53; *Kām. Nīti.*, 4, 50-56.
39. *Arth.*, II, 1.
40. *Yāj. Sm.*, 1, 318-20.
41. *Arth.*, II, 1.
42. *Mbh. Śānti Parva*, 88, 3-8; *Agn.*, 223, 1-5; *Viṣ. Sm.*, 3, 7-14; *Manu.*, VII, 115-17; *Viṣ. Dh. Pu.*; 2, 61, 1-6; *Mānaso.*, 2, 2, 159-62. See also *Ind. Ant.*, VIII, p. 20; 12, pp. 247-51; *Ep. Ind.*, XIV, p. 121.
43. *Mbh. Śānti Parva*, 88, 3-8; *Agn.*, 223, 4-5; *Viṣ. Sm.*, 3, 7-14; *Manu.*, VII, 16-17.
44. See both *Manu.*, VII, 118-19 and *Mbh. Śānti Parva*, 88, 6-8.
45. *Śuk. Nīti.*, 1, 191-92.
46. *Arth.*, II, 1.
47. *Manu.*, VII, 114.
48. *Arth.*, II, 35.
49. *Mbh. Śānti Parva*, 88, 9; *Manu.*, VII, 120.
50. *Mbh. Śānti Parva*, 69, 10; *Agn.*, 223, 2-3.
51. For details see *Yāj. Sm.*, 1.322; *Viṣ. Sm.* 3, 16.21; *Viṣ. Dh. Pu.*, 2.24, 148-49; *Manu.*, VII, 61 and 81; *Arth.*, 2, 9; *Kām. Nīti.*, 5, 75.
52. *Ep. Ind.*, XV, p. 113; XVII, p. 345 and 348; XXI, p. 78.
53. *Arth.*, II, 1.
54. *Mbh. Śānti Parva*, 60, 3; 67, 2-3; 73, 20; 88, 19-20; also 92, 22-23; *Mats.*, 220, 40-44; *Manu.*, VII, 110, 112-13.
55. *Mbh. Śānti Parva.*, 95, 3 and 5.
56. *Ibid.*, 67, 121; 73, 20-21.
57. *Ibid.*, 67, 5-8.
58. *Mbh. Śānti Parva*, 69, 59; 87, 30; *Viṣ. Sm.*, Ch. 3; *Manu.*, VII, 32, 68; IX, 312.

5

THE FORTS/CAPITAL (Durgas/Pura)

THE *Pura* (capital, *Nagara* or forts), as referred to in the *Mahābhārata*[1], was no less important than other organs of the state. Manu by placing *Pura* (which, according to commentator, Kullūka Bhatta, denotes both forts and fortified capital city) before *rāṣṭra* has accorded third place to it in the list of seven limbs of the state.[2] Actually, the *rāṣṭra* was composed of villages, towns and cities. The capital was, indeed, a pivotal point of the administrative machinery of whole state.

The importance of forts has also been highlighted by some political thinkers. According to Yājñavalkya, the safety of king and his subjects and treasury absolutely depends on the erection of strong forts.[3] The followers of the school of Ācārya Parāśara also consider *durgas* relatively more important than *Janapada*. While stating the reasons in support of their contention, they hold that the fort is necessary for deployment and protection of army as well as for protection of the treasury. This is also supported by Kauṭilya. It has been further observed by them that the forts in comparison to *nagara* and citizens serve more as an impregnable force and in emergency give shelter to everybody. The safety of whole *Janapada* or *rāṣṭra* depends on them.[4]

The king in order to build a *nagara* or capital for his own habitation had to choose a site which was located in beautiful natural surroundings, gifted with natural wealth, suitable for fortifications, inhabited more by *Vaiśyas, Śūdras*, artisans and craftsmen than the *Brāhmaṇs* and not conquerable by enemies, and where there were impregnable forts and whose inhabitants were dependable and invincible.[5]

It was advisable on the part of the king to construct a fort of his choice and to build his capital within its circumference.

The *Mahābhārata*,[6] some of the *Purāṇas*,[7] the *Smṛtis*[8] and *Śukranītisāra*[9] refer to the following six different types of *durgas* : (a) *Dhānva-durga* (constructed in a secluded place surrounded by desert or on the plain within the circumference of 5 *yojana*), (b) *Mahi-durga* (a fort made of stones or bricks), (c) *Jala-durga* (a fort constructed on the bank of river or a fort surrounded by water on all sides), (d) *Giri-durga* (a fort on the mountain or surrounded by mountains on all sides), (e) *Vana-durga* or *Briksha durga* (a fort constructed near forest or surrounded by trees on all sides up to one *yojana*) and (f) *Manuṣya* or *Nṛi-durga* (a fort protected by all four wings or army). In some of the texts[10] the *Giri-durga* has been considered the best among all from defensive point of view. Manu, in particular, has marked this *durga* as the most suitable for the dwelling of king. The king was supposed to build a *nagara* or his capital after constructing a particular fort from the point of view of his safety against enemy's attack.[11] One particular source[12] has mentioned nine *durgas* by adding three more (made of stones, bricks and clay) to aforesaid six *durgas*.

Kauṭilya, on the other hand, has referred to only four *durgas* : (1) *Audaka-durga* (surrounded by water on all four sides looking like a delta), (2) *Paravat-durga* (made on the mountains or made of rocks), (3) *Dhānvana-durga* (on the plain surrounded by desert) and (4) *Vana-durga* (near thick forest). The first two *durgas* were useful for protecting *Janapada* in case of emergency and the following two provided shelters to the king and others in the event of any emergency. It has also been said that on the frontiers of *Janapada* on all four sides the king should get such natural forts erected, which may be suitable particularly from the defensive point of view.[13]

The epic bears an eloquent testimony to the fact that Hastināpur[14] in the Kuru country, Dvārakā[15] in Saurāshṭra and Girivraja[16] (well protected by five mountains, *viz.* Vaihāra, Varāha, Vṛṣava, Ṛṣigiri and Cetya), the earliest capital of Magadha, were well fortified *nagaras*. Archaeological excavations and explorations at some ancient sites have already confirmed the literary evidence that some *nagaras* and cities were well fortified for the defence of the state or *rāṣṭra*.

The characteristic features of nagaras or capital cities are also described in different literary sources. On the whole, we find that they had very extensive frontiers. The areas covered was double or triple of a hundred *dhanusha* (=in distance=two hundred yards, which was the area of a village). They were surrounded by palisade walls, very high boundary walls and ditches. The well decorated gates including main gate, gorgeous, magnificent and towering buildings of a great height with minarets and domes, forts, markets, well planned streets, kings' and queens' palaces and other residential buildings constructed for ministers, *Purohitas*, physicians and other staffs, temples for worshipping gods and goddesses, assembly-hall, meeting places, etc. adorned the beauty of *nagaras*. They were peopled by king and his staffs, *Brāhmaṇs*, artisans, masons and others.

From the point of view of their defence the store-house (*Koshthāgara*) or treasury, magazines (*āyudhāgāra*), granary, armoury, different arms and weapons, war instruments, elephant force, cavalry, chariots, armed forces and king's friends were kept there.[17]

The defence of *nagaras* was a matter of principal concern for the king. In all the four sides of a fort ditches were dug and armed forces were placed to take care of. Besides main gates, many other small gates as passage for going out of *nagaras* were also built and well protected. At all the gates different weapons including cannons called "*Śataghni Topa*" suitable for killing hundred persons at a time and other fire-arms were placed. All other small forts, which provided shelters to the hostile forces, were demolished. A very strong wall for erecting fort was built. In order to watch the activities of enemies and for using missiles and firing shots at them several small holes in the walls of forts were made. For emergency purposes enough grains were stored inside the fort. The beggars, bullock-cart drivers and the drama-players were not allowed to settle in *nagaras*. But in the state capital

(*Rājanagari*) *nata*, *nartaka* (dancers), wrestlers, magicians and persons expert in deceptive arts were given shelter and kept happy. The king had also to take care of the people inhabiting *Puras* and *Śākhā-nagara* or a branch city. They were treated by the king like his sons but no partiality was extended to them. But in case of any doubt about their integrity the king had to adopt measures to keep them under control.[18]

The "*Dutas*" or ambassadors were sent to *Janapadas* and *nagaras* for collecting the detailed information about them.[19] The *durga* was one of those eight subjects (*āstavarga* including agriculture, trade, forests, mines, tunnel, etc.), which needed enough attention from the king.[20] The *Purāṇa* also refers to *durga-adhyakṣa*.[21] The cities or *nagaras* were governed by their own special officers holding a very high status. They exercised their control over the chiefs of villages too.[22] And their activities were watched by some ministers.[23]

Kauṭilya has provided an elaborate description of *nagaras*. According to him, the site for building *nagaras* should be selected in accordance with the advice of an expert on architectural engineering. He has also referred to *nagaras* built on the banks of ponds or reservoirs and on the confluence of rivers, the commercial towns and *sthāniya nagaras* (headquarters of 800 villages), the land and river routes, the trading centres, ditches, the walls made of stones and bricks, big houses with stairs, houses with separate apartments for women, separate places for armed forces, tunnels, a separate place for taking shelter, wall with holes (*niṣkuhdvāra*) for taking aim at enemies, a strong door gate consisting of six posts on a terrace near forts, different gates (*nagardvāra*), six roads divided into three each from east to west and from north to south, small streets, state place, *harem*, houses of *Purohitas*, ministers, *Yajñaśālā*, store-house, markets and shops, armoury, residential complexes for chief mason, *kṣatriyas, nagarā-dhyakṣa* (chief officer of *nagara*), *dhanyādhyakṣa* (incharge of treasury), *vyāpārādhyakṣa* (officer in charge of trade and commerce), inspectors of factories and army commander, temples of gods and goddesses, etc. The methods of constructing forts in *nagaras* corresponded to that applied for *durgas* on the frontiers of *Janapadas*. He has also pin-pointed that the king should not allow those people to settle in *nagaras* who may be instrumental in bringing the moral, religious and national standard of *nagaras* and *rāṣṭra* down. Such people should be made to settle on the frontiers and state tax be collected from them.[24]

NOTES AND REFERENCES

1. *Mbh. Śānti Parva*, 87, 1-3; also 69, 6-7.
2. *Manu.*, IX, 294.
3. *Yāj. Sm.*, 1, 321.
4. *Arth.*, VIII, 1.
5. *Mats.*, 217, 1-9; *Agn.*, 222, 1-4; *Manu.*, VII, 69; *Yāj. Sm.*, I, 321.
6. *Mbh. Śānti Parva*, 87, 4-5.
7. *Mats.*, 217, 6-7; *Agn.*, 222, 4-6; *Viṣ. Dh. Pu.*, 2, 26; 6-9; 3, 323, 16-21.
8. *Manu.*, VII, 70; *Viṣ. Sm.*, 3, 6.
9. *Suk. Nīti.*, 4, 6.
10. *Mats.*, 217, 7-9; *Agn.*, 222, 4-6; *Manu.*, VII, 71.
11. *Manu.*, VII, 72-73.
12. *Mānaso.*, 2, 5.
13. *Arth.*, 2, 3.

14. *Mbh. Āraṇyaka Parva*, 1, 8-9.
15. *Ibid.*, Chs. 15-16.
16. *Mbh. Sabhā Parva*, 19, 1-16.
17. *Mbh. Śānti Parva*, 87, 6-12; *Āshramavāsika Parva*, 9, 16-17; *Mats.*, 217, 10-26; 227, 24-25; *Agn.*, 222, 1-6; 227, 19-20; 239, 28-29; *Manu.*, VII, 75-76, IX, 264-66; 280 and 289; *Kām. Nīti.*, 4, 57-60; *Śuk. Nīti.*, 1, 213-17; 4, 612-13; *Viṣ. Dh. Pu.*, 2, 26, 20-88; *Mānaso.*, 3, 5, 550-55.
18. For details see *Mbh. Śānti Parva*, 69, 20, 25-26, 33-35, 39-59; also 59, 48; *Āshramavāsika Parva*, 9, 16-17; see also *Sabhā Parva*, 5, 25.
19. *Mbh. Śānti Parva*, 87, 15, 19-21.
20. *Agn.*, 239, 44-45.
21. *Mats.*, 215, 39.
22. *Manu.*, VII, 121-122; *Mbh. Śānti Parva*, 88, 10; *Arth.*, 2, 1.
23. *Mbh. Śānti Parva*, 88, 10.
24. *Arth.*, 2, 3-4.

6

THE TREASURY (Kosha)

IT was one of the six virtues as well as the primary duty of the king to replenish the treasury, amass the wealth by all pure means and to increase the resources of the state by collecting taxes from different sources for not only consolidating his own financial position, but also to promote the growth of the state and welfare of his subjects. The whole transaction of the state depended on *Kosha*. The revenue and the army were the twin pillars of all ancient Indian states. It was not possible for any king to exist with depleted treasury. Actually, the *Kosha* was the root of the tree of state.[1] It has been rightly said that "*yatra rāja tatra koṣaḥ koṣādhīnā hi rājatā.*" Thus, "where there is a king, there is *kosha* . . . ."[2] About its importance Ācārya Piśuna (Nārada) has said that the protection of *durgas* solely depends on *Kosha*. Any crisis confronting the *Janapadas* and friends can be averted and the defeat of enemies can also be ensured with its help. The kings of other states can also be persuaded on its strength to render the assistance sought for. The use of armed forces also depends on it. In case of emergency the treasury can be shifted from one place to another, but same cannot be done in case of *durgas*. Kauṭilya, while admitting its importance, has also emphasized the fact that in absence of *Kosha* the army cannot do anything rather they can go against their own king and join the hostile forces. He considers both *Kosha* and army equally important, but comparatively the former is more important than the latter. He says that the army protects only *Kosha*, but the latter protects both army and *durgas*.[3]

It has been said that the king should go on collecting the taxes from his subjects according to the rules prescribed in *Śāśtra*.[4] But, on the other hand, the king has been permitted to accumulate wealth by applying three methods, *i.e. Sām, Dām* and *Bheda*. Bṛhaspati has pointed out that the king should remain contented with whatever wealth he has in his possession.[5]

The king generally used to collect one-sixth of the income or produce of his subjects as tax.[6] But in case of emergency, particularly in the event of war, the king was at liberty to collect heavy taxes from his subjects.[7] But before doing so the people had to be informed about the nature of emergency and the necessity of collecting taxes from them. It was the duty of the king of take his subjects into confidence about the collection of extra taxes from them. He had to declare that in order to protect the state and the people from enemy there is necessity of collecting taxes. The king had also to convince them that for averting the national crisis the taxes will be collected according to their capacity and they will not be subjected to any harassment. Thereafter, an officer was deputed and instructed to collect emergency taxes from them without exploiting them.[8] According to Kauṭilya, in case of an economic crisis also the king had to collect the extra taxes from the people. One-third or one-fourth of the total produce of big, medium and small *Janapadas* was collected as taxes. But the *Janapadas* situated on the frontiers or with little produce or useful for economic and commercial purposes were not supposed to pay state tax. One-fourth of the land produce and one-sixth of the forest produce were also taken as taxes. One-fiftieth of the total cost on the commercial products like gold, silver, diamond, pearls, etc., one-fortieth of cotton clothes, metals, herbs, etc., one-thirtieth of crops like wheat and oil, ghee, iron etc., one-twentieth of income from big merchants and artisans and one-tenth of income from small artisans and one-fifth of woods, bamboos, stones, earthen ware, etc. were collected as state taxes. But it was collected only once and not twice.[9] From other sources also it appears that the taxes were collected annually.[10] The treatment meted out to the people was generally good. Subjects were not put to any torture.

According to Manu, the king used to receive taxes from the traders and merchants. The king had to take into consideration the productivity of the soil and labour of the farmer before collecting either one-sixth or one-eight or one-twelfth of the total produce. He used to get one-fiftieth of the income obtained from animal husbandry. He had to get one-sixth of honey, ghee, medicinal herbs, salt, fruits, vegetables, skins etc. in the form of tax.[11] According to Kullūka, the king used to appoint one chief officer called "*adhyakṣa*" to look after *Kosha* on behalf of the king.[12] The king was himself in-charge of finance or *Kosha* and state.[13] The finance department had to deal with revenue collection and taxation.

The king used to impose very mild tax, particularly on the *Vaiśyas* or traders, because the agricultural and commercial progress of the state very much depended on them.[14] While collecting the taxes from the *rāṣṭra* (which has been compared to a cow), it was the special duty of the king to keep the interest of his subjects in mind. He was not supposed to collect enough taxes from his subjects except for emergency.[15] The custodians of *Pura* were also supposed to contribute little to the richness of the treasury.[16] It has been pin-pointed that while collecting taxes from artisans, craftsmen, traders, agriculturists or the subjects as a whole, they should not be exploited, otherwise, the whole *rāṣṭra* will fall in the grip of poverty.[17]

The king used to collect one-twentieth of saleable commodities as tax. But, while determining the tax structure, particularly in respect of imported goods the king had to take into account the total cost of the items, the total profits of the traders and the cost of damage, if any. This kind of tax was nowhere more than one-twentieth of the total goods. The king had to collect one-sixth or one-eighth of the income of those traders who evaded payment of taxes or custom duties. Generally, one-fifth or one-sixth part of most of the items was collected as tax.[18]

Kauṭilya makes mention of *Saṇṇidhāta* (*Koshādhyakṣa*), whose duty was to set up '*Koshagriha*' or treasury-house.[19] In order to increase the resources, the king was supposed to augment the wealth of the whole *rāṣṭra*, to encourage all kinds of production, to promote trade and commerce, to collect taxes in time, etc. The *Koshādhyakṣa* was not supposed to violate the rules regarding the collection of state taxes. He was not supposed to make any mistake regarding the handling of state taxes. In case of not depositing it in the treasury or misusing it for his personal gain or not collecting taxes regularly or taking bribes from the subjects or terrorizing them or reducing the amount of taxes or not maintaining the account properly, etc. he was severely punished. He could be punished for any one of the eight kinds of mistake mentioned in the text.[20]

The chief sources of income of the state were the king's share of the land produce, customs duties and the amout collected as fines. The main tax payers were the farmers, traders and artisans. Generally the king used to collect one-sixth, one-eighth or one-twelfth of the land produce. The goods brought either by land or sea-routes were subjected to tax. The fines were imposed on defaulters or culprits.

The king was entitled to take one-fourth (in normal case) and one-eighth (in case of an emergency) of the income of the *Vaiśyas*, and one-twentieth of gold and silver as taxes. He was not supposed to collect taxes from the *Śūdras*, carpenters and others, who offered their services to the state as a labour.[21] The treasury fully replenished with different kinds of wealth, gold, silver and precious gems, and providing protection to all the subjects in emergency, was called *Rājakosha*.[22]

Thus, stating the matters precisely we can say that different ways and means were adopted to increase the resources of the state.

NOTES AND REFERENCES

1. *Mbh. Śānti Parva*, 57, 18; 87, 20; 108, 2-3; 116, 119; 119, 16; 128, 35-36; *Āshramavāsika Parva*, 10, 9; *Agn.*, 239, 30, 43,

46-48; *Arth.*, 2, 8; *Manu.*, VII, 65; *Kām. Nīti.*, 5, 77; 13, 33; *Śuk. Nīti.*, 1, 276-78; *Viṣ. Dh. Pu.*, 2, 61, 17; *Yāj. Sm.*, I, 327-38.

2. *Agn.*, 242, 33.
3. *Arth.*, VIII, 1.
4. *Agn.*, 223, 13.
5. *Mbh. Śānti Parva*, 69, 23.
6. *Ibid.*, 69, 24; *Manu.*, VII, 130; *Viṣ. Sm.*, 3, 22-23; *Gau. Dh. Sū.*, 10-24.
7. *Mbh. Śānti Parva*, 88, 21-23; 128, 30-31, 38, 47; *Āshramavāsika Parva*, II, 8; *Manu.*, X, 118; VII, 213; *Arth.*, 5, 2; *Śuk. Nīti.*, 4, 2, 9-10.
8. *Mbh. Śānti Parva*, 88, 21-32; 128, 30-32, 38, 47, 49.
9. *Arth.*, 5, 2.
10. *Mats.*, 215, 57; *Manu.*, VII, 80 and 129.
11. *Manu.*, VII, 127-28, 130-32.
12. *Ibid.*, VII, 81.
13. *Ibid.*, VII, 65.
14. *Mbh. Śānti Parva*, 88, 33-36.
15. *Ibid.*, 89, 1-11 and 15.
16. *Ibid.*, 69, 25.
17. *Ibid.*, 88, 11-15.
18. *Agn.*, 223, 23-29.
19. *Arth.*, 2, 5.
20. For details see, *ibid.*, 2, 8.
21. Kullūka, *Manu.*, X, 120.
22. *Arth.*, VI, 1.

7

THE ARMY (Daṇḍa/Bala)

THERE is no unanimity of opinion among ancient political thinkers about the composition of army and its wings. However, from some literary sources it is quite evident that the soldiers recruited in the army belonged to the following six categories : (1) *Maula* (recruited on hereditary ground; permanent wing, maintained by state and whose duty was to defend the capital), (2) *Bhṛtaka* or *Bhṛta* (paid), (3) *Shreṇī* (a well-organised group of soldiers well trained in the art of war), (4) *Mitra* (soldiers of friendly kings), (5) *Amitra* (soldiers of hostile kings or of conquered countries and recruited like slaves) and (6) *Ātavi* or *Ātavika* (tribal soldiers consisting of *Niṣādas*, *Mlecchas* and other mountain tribes).[1] Kauṭilya, in particular, has added one more to the above list, that is (7) *Autsāhika* (living in different countries, without any leader and invaders). They used to attack other countries with or without the consent of king. Out of the above seven categories of soldiers the first three have been considered dependable.[2] The virtual existence of such soldiers in ancient India can be proved by an epigraphic evidence. The Maliya copper-plate of Mahārāja Dharasena II (*Vallabhi Saṁvat* 252=571-72 A.D.) shows that *Bhatārka*, the founder of Vallabhi state, was greatly helped by first four groups of soldiers as mentioned above in bringing the state under his rule.[3]

The six wings of the army as mentioned in the *Purāṇa*[4] and *Kāmandaka Nītisāra*[5] are the following : Infantry, cavalry, elephant force, chariot, *mantra* (policy) and *kosha*. Quite different from it, the *Mahābhārata* refers to the eight wings of army (*Aṣtānga Bala*), which are infantry, cavalry, elephants, chariot, boat, intelligence, unpaid carriers and the subjects. Further, it has been made clear that the seven limbs of the state (*Sapta-prakṛti*) and the army well equipped with all its wings, etc. go together to constitute the eight organs of the body politic.[6] It is perhaps on this ground that the state has also been called "*Aṣtāṅga-rājya*".[7] But, *daṇda* (army) has been considered the chief organ of the state.[8] Actually, the army consisted mainly of the infantry, cavalry, elephant force and chariots, called "*Caturaṅgaṇi sena*".[9]

The soldiers were recruited on the basis of their qualities like competence, efficiency, faithfulness, etc. The seniority, juniority and other criterias were also applied. They were recruited according to the needs of each department of the army and for the purpose of suppressing the hostile forces.[10]

Kauṭilya, while referring to the qualities of soldiers, has observed that they should be valiant warriors, well versed in the art of war, and loyal to the king. He has also mentioned that there should be maximum number of *Kṣatriyas* in the army. The soldiers should be recruited on the hereditary ground and on the permanent basis. In the event of war they may be well-equipped with all necessary things and they should fight bravely and crush the enemies.[11] He does not agree with all those *Ācāryas* who suggested that in comparison to the *Vaiśyas* and *Śūdras*, the *Brāhmaṇs* and *Kṣatriya* soldiers are more efficient. Quite contrary to it, he considers the *Kṣatriya* soldiers as the best, but does not deny that the *Vaiśyas* and *Śūdras* may also prove their worth provided they have some brave fighters or chivalrous persons among them. He holds that the hostile forces by submitting before the *Brāhmaṇs* or prostrating at their feet or bowing down before them easily win over them.[12] Śukra has also stated that the *Kṣatriyas, Vaiśyas, Śūdras* and *Mlecchas* may be recruited as soldiers.[13]

The *Senāpati* (commander-in-chief of the army) generally belonged to the *Kṣatriya* caste.[14] But there are also contradictory evidences to show that the king had the option to appoint the *Senāpati* either from amongst the *Brāhmanas* or the *Kṣatriyas*.[15] Manu has referred to both *Senāpati* and *Balādhyakṣa* (General).[16] The *Senāpati* was head of *daṇḍa* consisting of all the four wings, i.e. infantry, cavalry, chariots and elephants. The military department was also under the supervision of one *amātya* or minister and the ambassador of king was responsible for peace and war.[17] The opinions of experts on *Daṇḍaśāstra* show that he, who possessed adequate knowledge of all the six elements of state polity and war strategy, was endowed with commanding power and leadership qualities and had enough experience of fighting in the war, was appointed as chief of the army.[18] Each wing of the army was placed in the charge of suitable persons. The in-charge of weapons was designated as "*Astrācārya*".[19] The armoury, stable, the army cantonments, elephants, trench, etc. were kept in a secret place.[20]

The state without *bala* (army) was not in a position to provide security to the people and to maintain its existence. Thus, the army was deployed on the frontiers of the state and in villages, *nagaras* and *puras* or towns and cities, and near state palace. Apart from infantry and other wings of the army, the people from intelligence department also used to render very useful services to the state. The intelligence people were kept in *pura*, *janapadas* and near the territory ruled by *Sāmants* or feudatory rulers. The markets, public places, official residences, public roads, state assembly, etc. were kept under strict vigilance to watch the activities of enemies.[21]

It was the bounden duty of the king to crush the hostile forces. The king generally used to attack those states whose kings were very weak. But, on the other hand, he liked to enter into treaty of friendship with those who happened to be stronger than him. It was the duty of the king first to avert the possibility of war in the interest of the state. But in case of war all the soldiers had to take part in it. The chief officers of the army were sent to all secret and inaccessible places to collect the relevant information. A game was also played by the people living adjacent to the frontiers of the state to join the hands of friendship with hostile king and to expel the enemy from their country with the help of his army.[22] The soldiers had to fight under the command of *Senāpati*. The victorious army was also rewarded by the king. The war and diplomacy were the two chief political instruments for the king to keep his adversaries always under check.[23]

Manu has thrown enough light on the importance of *daṇḍa* for the king so far as the protection of the people and the defence of *rāṣṭra* are concerned.[24] He says that the king finding his opponent more stronger than him should divide his army into two parts, and should place one under *Senāpati* to crush the enemy and other in forts or other secured places for his own protection.[25] If all his attempts fail to save him, he should take shelter of more powerful king than himself.[26]

Ācārya Kauṇapadanta as well as Kauṭliya have pointed out that on the strength of a well organised army not only a friend of the king continues to be a friend but even an enemy is converted into a friend. The army and friends have been considered very helpful bodies for the king and, particularly in comparison to *Kosha,* the army has been considered more important limb of the state.[27]

NOTES AND REFERENCES

1. *Agn.*, 242, 1-2; *Arth.*, 9, 2; *Kām. Nīti.*, 18, 4, 5-9; *Mānaso.*, 2, 6, 556-60.
2. *Arth.*, 9, 2.
3. Quoted in P.V. Kane, *op. cit.*, p. 678.
4. *Agn.*, 242, 2-3.
5. *Kām. Nīti.*, 18, 24.
6. *Mbh. Śānti Parva*, 121, 42-46.
7. *Mbh. Āshramavāsika Parva*, 9, 8.
8. *Mbh. Śānti Parva*, 121, 44, 46.
9. *Agn.*, 228, 1-8; 242, 28-31; 35-40; *Arth.*, X, 4; *Manu.*, VII, 167.

10. *Arth.*, 9, 2.
11. *Ibid.*, VI, 1.
12. *Ibid.*, 9, 2.
13. *Śuk. Nīti.*, 2, 137-39.
14. *Agn.*, 239, 31-33.
15. *Mats.*, 215, 8-10; *Agn.*, Ch. 220.
16. *Manu.*, VII, 189.
17. *Manu.*, VII, 65.
18. *Mats.*, 215, 8-10; *Agn.*, 239, 31-33; 242, 4-6.
19. *Mats.*, 215, 16-21, 36-42.
20. *Mbh. Śānti Parva*, 69, 52-53.
21. *Ibid.*, 67, 2; 69, 6-12; *Manu.*, VII, 102, 167.
22. *Ibid.*, 69; 13-22, 36-38.
23. See *Agn.*, 242, 4, 20, 25-27, 32-72.
24. *Manu.*, VII, 14-18, 21-22, 27-32, 102, 169-70, 171-72, 173-89.
25. *Manu.*, VII, 173 and 184.
26. *Manu.*, VII, 174.
27. *Arth.*, VIII, 1.

8

THE ALLIES AND THE INTER-STATE RELATIONS (Mitra tathā Nīti)

THE three different manifestations of the ally, as found in ancient Indian literary texts, are Mitra (friends), *Suhṛda* (well-wisher) and *Sahāya* (helper).

The importance of *mitra* as one of the seven organs of a state can best be qualified in the following words of Manu. The king with land and gold cannot make as much progress as he can with the help of dependable friends.[1] Yājñavalkya also holds more or less the same view.[2] The land, gold and friendship are considered to be the products of war and diplomacy respectively.[3]

The paramount necessity of an ally for a king has been felt in all ages. The epic at one particular place has changed the sequence or the order of the said organs and put the *Mitra* at the top and the king at the end.[4] It was indispensable for a king to make friends and to enjoy the confidence of allies for taking all kinds of help and advice from them, so as to achieve the goal, that was the prosperity of his state.[5] The king without friends can easily fall prey to enemies' attack.[6]

Therefore, he should keep ministers and friends.[7] A king by increasing the number of friends can overcome all the problems and subdue his enemies.[8] In absence of treasury and friends the king can sustain an irreparable loss.[9]

The qualities and characteristics of true friends as well as the types of allies are indescribable. However, a brief and graphic picture of the subject can be presented here.

It has been emphatically asserted that a king should make those persons as his friends who are honest, truthful, grateful, hard-working, brave, liberal, softspoken, followers of justice, gifted with persuasive eloquence, expert in the science of knowledge, worthy of helping him in times of adversity and sharing his sorrow and pleasure, fit to maintain secrecy, etc.[10] He should not befriend those who are wicked, cruel, lazy, greedy and non-followers of *Dharma*; whose conduct is not satisfactory and who maintain adversaries and do not show respect to the inhabitants of *Puras*.[11]

In most of the texts we come across the description of four types of allies. In this connection the epic provides two different lists of friends. According to one list, those four types of allies known as natural friends are friends acquired by conciliatory words, friends won by offering financial assistance, friends made by showing one's own powers, etc.[12] The other four types of friends are those, who have the identical goal to achieve; those, who are seekers of shelter and protection; those, who are natural friends (*Sahaja*) and those, who are won over or acquired by offering something (*Kṛtrima*).[13] Besides, there is a separate category of friends called *Dharmātmā-Mitra* or the righteous friends, who follow right path and do not favour immoral friends.[14] It has been pointed out that *Bhajamāna* (ancestral or traditional) and *Sahaja* (acquired through relations) types are the best allies, but *Kṛtrima* (artificial) and *Sahārtha* are the worst or undependable, as the basis of their friendship is only the fulfilment of their self-interest.[15]

One of the *Purāṇas* also furnishes a list of four types of friends, who are – (1) *Ōrasa* (ancestral or descendants of kith and kin), (2) *Saṅaddha* (very close associate), (3) *Vaṁśakramānugāmi* (those who are in hereditary line) and (4) those who are prepared to help the king.[16] The *Purāṇic* list tallies with that of *Kāmandaka*, so far as the first and third category of friends are concerned. The two other friends as referred to by him are *'maitrasambaddham'* or *'kṛtasambaddham'* (friends acquired on the basis of matrimonial relationship) and *'Rakṣita'* (he who is protected from danger).[17] Friends are further classified into three groups, i.e. ancestral or traditional, feudatories of enemies and acquired (*Kṛtrima*).[18]

Kauṭilya has described six types of friends in connection with the *Saptāṅga* theory : (1) traditional, (2) permanent, (3) who could exercise restraint upon himself, (4) who is not of hostile attitude, (5) who is endowed with courage and ability to offer worthy advice and (6) those, who could help in need. A friend equipped with all these qualities was, indeed, a real friend.[19]

The epic enjoins the king to keep his friends not only in his own *rāṣṭra*, but also in other's *rāṣṭra* (*rājya*), in the *nagaras* of *māndalika*, feudatories or *Sāmanta rāja*, in the forest areas, etc.[20] The well wishers and the most faithful among the friends are said to be employed by the king to inspect the salt and gold mines and the markets and other trading centres.[21]

They had to perform manifold duties for the king. One of their primary duties was to advise the king regarding his political relations with the kings of neighbouring states. The king used to consult them before entering into any alliance or concluding a treaty of friendship with more powerful king than himself. In case of any trouble created by other powerful king he had also to seek their advice for his self-defence.[22] It has also been mentioned that the allies should protect each other from destruction on the basis of their mutual co-operation.[23] The allies had to play an important role in the spheres of mutual relations of kings by strictly adhering to the principles of check and balance.

In this connection various other types of friends and enemies have been described, some of which are worthy of our attention. The three noted friends were called *Sahaja-mitra* (obtained through near relatives), *Kṛtrima* (acquired by virtue of obliging other king or being obliged by the latter) and *Prākṛta* (living adjacent to the frontiers of neighbouring king). Likewise the three kinds of enemies were called *Sahaja Śatru* (found among own relatives), *Kṛtrima Śatru* (always hostile to others) and *Prakṛta Śatru* (neighbouring kings).[24]

"Enemies are further divided into three categories, i.e. (1) ancestral (*kulya*), (2) immediate neighbour (*anantara*) and acquired (*kṛtrima*) and each one of them is comparatively more dangerous than the succeeding one."[25] Kāmandaka and Somadeva Suri also mention two types of enemies, ancestral (*Sahaja*) and artificial or acquired (*Kṛtrima*).[26]

"This categorisation of friends and foes . . . points to three important principles of inter-state relationship. First, ties of blood relationship are valued much. Secondly, immediate neighbouring states are considered to be always hostile to one another. Thirdly, . . . the feudatory states are generally treated as inimical to their overlords. All these hypotheses lead us to think of a state of affairs in which states being obsessed with the idea of self-aggrandisement are in perpetual hostility to one another, and the state reduced to the position of vassals desire to regain their freedom with the connivance of kings opposed to their overlords."[27]

The king in order to conquer his enemies had to take help of his friends. The whole system of inter-state relations in ancient India was based on the equation which a king maintained with his friends and the attitude and policies which he adopted towards his foes. The political ideas intimately associated with the inter-relations of the states led to the formulation of a theory in the epic age, which later became popularly known as the *Maṇḍala* theory. This theory seeks further explanations and fresh interpretation.

From the *Śānti Parva* of the *Mahābhārata* it distinctly appears that it was first explained in the original code of *Nītiśāstra of Brahmā.* A *maṇḍala* consisting of four different kinds of friends (*mitra*), enemies (*śatru*) and *udāsina* (neutral kings)=4x3=12, has been called "*Dvādaśarājikā*", which denotes a circle of twelve kings ruling over twelve different types of states, i.e. *Dvādaśrājamandal.* The king, the methods for promoting the growth of state and the means of protecting the inhabitants of *Pur*, etc. also figure in his code. This finds reflection in the following verses :

रक्षणं चैव पौशणां स्वराष्ट्रस्य विबर्धनम ।
मण्डलस्था च या चिन्ता राजन्द्वादशराजिका ॥[28]

The *manḍala* theory as such was first formulated in the age of *Mahābhārata*. From the epic it is quite evident that twelve different types of king, the '*Shāḍ-guṇya*' (six fold stages of diplomacy), friends, enemies and others called '*parkiya*', '*ātamiya*', '*udāsina*' and '*madhyama*', the allies of a king, enemy of his ally, friend of his friend and enemy of his friends, mutual relations of kings, alliances, treaty, diplomacy, the growth and decline of the state, etc. form the subject matter of *rājamanḍal*. The king had to be very careful of all his friends, enemies and others, who constituted the *manḍal* of twelve kings.[29]

This theory is directly related to the growth and welfare of the *Saptāṇga* state, which can be fairly proved by the following *Purāṇic* evidence :

वक्ष्ये मण्डलचिन्तां ते कर्त्तव्यं राजरक्षणम् ॥
स्वाम्यमात्यस्तथा दुर्गः कोषो दण्डस्थैव च ।
मित्रं जनपदश्चैव राज्यं सप्ताङ्गमुच्यते ॥
सप्ताङ्गस्य तु राज्यस्य विघ्नकर्तृन्विनाशयेत् ।
मण्डलेषु च सर्वेषु वृद्धिः कार्यामहीक्षिता ॥[30]

Placing our reliance on the combined testimony of the epic,[31] the *Purāṇas*,[32] *Arthaśāstra* of Kauṭilya,[33] *Smṛtis*,[34] Kāmandaka's *Nītisāra*,[35] *Nītivākyāmṛta*,[36] *Rājnītiprakāśa*,[37] *Rājanītimayukha*,[38] *Mānasollasa*[39] and other sources,[40] we can have a clearer picture of the subject concerned. From all these sources it appears that the *manḍala* consisted of following twelve kings : (1) *Vijigishu*—one who seeks conquest to expand the frontiers of his state; a powerful and ambitious king ruling over the state equipped with all seven organs, (2) *Ari*—the enemy in front of No. 1, or the hostile king living in the neighbourhood of No. 1, (3) *Mitra*—an ally ruling over the state adjacent to *Ari*, (4) *Ari-Mitra*—an ally of *Ari* in front of No. 3, (5) *Mitra-mitra*—friend of friend or an ally of No. 3 in front of No. 4, (6) *Arimitra-mitra*—friend of enemy's friend or an ally of No. 4 in front of No. 5, (7) *Pārshnigraha*—rearward enemy in the rear of No. 1 or an enemy who suddenly attacks No. 1, (8) *Ākranda*—an ally ruling over the state in front of No. 7 or friend of No. 1 and enemy of No. 7, (9) *Pārshnigrāhasāra*—ally of No. 7 in front of No. 8, (10) *Ākrandasāra*—ally of No. 8 in front of No. 9, (11) *Madhyama*—an intermediate king occupying a territory close to both the conqueror (*Vijigishu*) and his immediate enemy in front (*ari*) and he can help or resist either of them, and (12) *Udāsina*— neutral king or a king either in front of No. 1 or ruling over the state far from that of No. 1, but in any case remains indifferent to him (*Vijigishu*).

Ācarya Uddhava or Vātavyādhi has attached greater importance to *mitra* than army. He observes that *mitra*, in spite of living in a far-flung area, works for *Vijigishu* and counteracts *Pārśnigraha* (the king who suddenly attacks on other's state) and his friends, other enemies and *atāvika* force (tribal rulers ruling over the forest kingdoms). He concludes that the allies always help *Vijigishu* through the resources, army and territory at their disposal. They do not desert him even in crisis.[41]

All the above twelve kings on the basis of their

alignment can be divided into following three groups : (a) *Vijigishu, ari, Madhyama* and *Udāsina*, (b) *mitra, mitra-mitra, ākranda* and *ākrandasāra* and (c) *ari-mitra, ari-mitra-mitra, pārshnigraha* and *pārshnigrahasāra*.

All the twelve kings (friends and foes) forming the *rāja-maṇḍala* (confederation of twelve kings) are considered equivalent to twelve *prakṛtis*, which is collectively known as '*rāja-prakṛti*'. Each one of them has five elements : (1) *amātya*, (2) territory, (3) forts, (4) treasury and (5) army. Thus, 12x5=60 are '*dravya-prakṛti*'. These sixty *prakṛtis* added to twelve (60+12) become 72 *prakṛtis*, which constitute the basis of *rājamandal*. The statements of Kauṭilya[42] and Manu[43] in regard to the *Saptāṅga* theory of the state are in perfect agreement with each other. The statements made by *Uśanā*,[44] *Kāmandaka*[45] and *Daṇḍin*[46] go directly or indirectly to corroborate the views of both Kauṭilya and Manu. The number of *prakṛtis* go up to 108,[47] however, it is 72 *prakṛtis* which figure in all the authentic texts.

The focus of *mandal* theory is not only on the inter-state relations but also on the *Shāḍgunya* (six-fold stages of diplomacy), which are the following : (1) *saṅdhi* (alliance), (2) *Vigraha* (war or hostility), (3) *Yāna* (expedition or march of the army), (4) *Āsana* (neutrality), (5) *Saṁsrya* (seeking shelter or a weak king seeking protection of stronger king) and (6) *Dvaidhibhāva* (duplicity or dual policy).[48] The *Mahābhārata*, besides the *Shāḍgunya*, also refers to *trivarga—briddhi* (growth), *kṣaya* (decay) and *sthān*, and *param-tribarga—dharma, artha* and *kāma* (6+3+3=12), which a king must follow.[49] Further, on the basis of *Shāḍguṇya* and *dvādaśa-rājamandal* the *Mahābhārata* refers to total 72 (12x6=72) *prakṛtis*.[50]

Romila Thapar has rightly pointed out that the "*Mandal* theory" represents "mathematically balanced diplomacy".[51]

The importance of the above statements lies in the fact that the kings and the *Saptāṅga* state were inter-dependent. The success of one depended on the other. The *Shāḍguṇya* (six different policies framed on the basis of diplomacy), as already mentioned, were pre-requisite conditions for striking balance in the inter-relations of the state. Thus, these six policies constituted the pillars of the edifice of the *Saptāṅga* state. Moreover, the said circle of twelve kings had to take care of the constituents of their respective states and watch the activities of their respective friends and foes. The king had to act with the help of allies as well as six policies. Thus, the so-called seventy two *prakṛtis* comprising the kings and constituents of the states form an important part of ancient Indian polity and administration.

The concept of *Maṇḍala* envisages mutual relationship between different states. It was the duty of the king to exterminate all those forces which proved stumbling block in the way of progress of the *Saptāṅga* state. He has been exhorted to increase the number of his friends and well wishers and to watch the activities of all those who were hostile to him. A strong king had to conquer the state of a weak king. If a king was not in a strong position, he had to conclude treaty with his enemies. If oppressed by a stronger king the weaker king had to enter into mutual consultation with his friends in accordance with the idea embodied in so-called *tri-varga*. The divide and rule policy was to be followed among the allies of an anemy. The people inhabiting the frontier of a state were supposed to extend the hands of friendship with enemies for driving them away from their states with the help of their own army.[52]

According to the principles of the *Maṇḍala* theory, the different states had to determine their attitude towards their neighbours in time of war according to their own convenience or in accordance with the principle of expediency. As for example, if war broke out between the *Vijigishu* and his immediate neighbour in front (*Ari*-enemy), it was not necessary for the *mitra* to extend his help to *Vijigishu*. Because, he had to determine his attitude after taking into consideration his own advantages and disadvantages and other factors such as the power and strength of the foe of his friend and the prospect of success of *Vijigishu*. So the policy of hostility towards the *Ari* or *Vijigishu* was not always applied. Likewise the *Udāsina* and *Madhyama* kings also adopted an attitude of indifference and neutrality towards parties engaged in a mutual conflict. The principle of *maṇḍala* theory was not followed in a uniform fashion in the epic age. The Matshya king, Virāta, in spite of being immediate neighbour of the Kauravas, was their enemy. But, on the other hand, the Trigartas, the immediate neighbour of king Virāta, were friends of Kauravas. The Kshudraka and Mālavās were the immediate neighbours, but they were always on friendly terms being the member of a confederate state.[53] The *Mitra* and *Ari* were the two main aspects of the system of inter-state relations.

Out of the six types of diplomacy war and peace

were very important. Kāmandaka has mentioned following sixteen types of treaties : (1) treaty with equal (*kapāla*), (2) treaty negotiated with gifts (*upahāra*), (3) matrimonial alliance (*santāna*), (4) treaty of friendship (*saṅgata*), (5) treaty to achieve something good (*upanyāsa*), (6) treaty for mutual help (*pratikāra*), (7) treaty for joint venture to achieve some aim (*saṁyoga*), (8) treaty to gain something through their chiefs of the armies (*purusāntara*), (9) treaty with one who makes agreement with enemies (*adṛṣṭanara*), (10) treaty after offering land (*ādiṣṭa*), (11) compact with his own army (*ātmā*), (12) purchasing safety of life at all cost (*upagraha*), (13) treaty after offering money to protect his kingdom (*parikrama*), (14) treaty at the cost of fertile land (*chhina*), (15) treaty after offering all the land produce (*paradūsana* or *paribhūṣana*) and (16) treaty after offering some fruits to be placed on shoulders of servants (*skandhopaneya*).[54] The mutual relations of states were also governed by the nature of treaty, which they concluded with each other.

The inter-state relations in ancient India were also regulated by different ways and means termed as '*upāya*' or expedients. The seven expedients, as stated in the *Purāṇa*, are conciliation or persuasion, gift, dissension, punishment, indifference (*upekṣā*), illusion and magical tricks.[55] A ruler had to subbue his enemies by following the policy of conciliation or persuasion, by offering financial assistance, by pacifying them or creating dissension, by the use of force, by creating illusions with or without magical tricks, by adopting the policy of neutrality or by remaining indifferent, etc.

Thus, we find that inter-state relation in ancient

India was broadly based on three traditional principles : the *maṇḍala* theory or the theory of circle of twelve states, the *Shāḍguṇya* or six fold policy and the seven *upāyas* or expedients.

After having made a thorough analysis of the data contained in the sources concerned, we find that the *Maṇḍala* theory is largely based on the doctrine of 'balance of power' and the *Shāḍguṇya*—a charter of policies prepared by ancient political thinkers for the king to follow and act upon. The growth and decline of the state are completely based on this theory. The friendship among the few rulers of the state is bound to result in the formation of another group joined by like-minded kings. Thus, there will be division of *rājamandal* into two blocks—*mitra-rāṣṭra* and *śatru-rāṣṭra* (or allied group of friendly states and rival group of enemies' states). This is what it gets reflected in various statements. The king, therefore, has to remain alert in identifying his friends and enemies. The six different kinds of policies, which he was supposed to adopt, were the protection of the people, increase of resources, employment of faithful ministers, formation of alliance with friendly states, war with hostile group of kings and the defence of forts, *Janapadas*, etc. He should carefully identify his four kinds of friends, four kinds of enemies and four kinds of *Udāsina*, whose states lie far beyond the state of a conqueror and who is indifferent to latter. He should watch the activities of friends of his friend (*mitra-mitra*), friends of friends of enemies (*ari-mitra-mitra*), etc. *Sāmantas*, loyal to the king, should be taken as friend and if hostile to him as enemy. A king seeking conquest must remain always cautious. He should distinguish between the friends and foes, among his ministers, among those living in *Janapadas*, *Pur* and forts and among the members of the armed forces. He should declare war against the weak king and if his position is shaky, he should enter into alliance with stronger king than him. For the progress of the state credit will go to the king and for decline the whole responsibilities will devolve upon him. The whole structure of modern international diplomacy seems to be based on this ancient theory.

This theory is said to be "the most notable contributions of the ancient Indians to the development of the world political thought.[56]

Each and every king was supposed to rule over his own state and to adopt all measures to protect it against hostile forces. It has been stated that a king (*Vijigishu*) should neither capture the territory of the conquered state nor its citizens, wealth and the sons and daughters of the conquered king. Rather, the conqueror should take the responsibilities of protecting the conquered state like that of his own state, preserving its tradition, customs and culture and maintaining its identity. He should not wipe out the existence of such state. He should allow either the son of the deceased king or his kith and kin to succeed to the throne. He should not impose any other king on the vacant throne. He should restore all other persons of the conquered state to their former positions, He should maintain cordial relations with the newly appointed king of such a state. He should see that the administration of the conquered state is run peace-fully, so that there could be stability in the administration. On the contrary to it, if a conqueror takes the king of the conquered state into custody or kills him and thereafter takes into his possession its territory, wealth and the sons and wives of the king, the whole *rājamandal* goes against him. In the event of such happenings the council of ministers and other high officials of the conqueror join the hostile group of kings because of disgustment and vindictive attitude. There seems to be a consensus of opinion among Vālmīki,[57] Vyāsa,[58] Kauṭilya,[59] Manu,[60] Purāṇakāra,[61] *Smṛti- kāras* or writers of *Dharmaśāsras*[62] and others[63] in this regard.

The above seems to be a unique and splendid example of cordial behaviour of a conqueror towards the conquered state. Such ideals were maintained by the conquerors of ancient times. For instance, Rudradāman and Samudragupta had acknowledged the claims of the former kings of the conquered states. Such example, as presented in ancient India, perhaps goes without parallel in the history of ancient civilizations of other countries of the world.

Manu speaks of '*Śvarāṣṭra*' (own state) and '*Pararāja*' (others' state),[64] which proves that there were more than one state in Āryāvarta during his time. It was the duty of the king to watch the activities of neighbouring states and to punish the offenders of his own state as well as that of others.

The *Mahābhārata* also refers to the duty of the king to take care of enemies in both '*Svarājya*' and '*Pararājya*'.[65]

It appears that the traditional theory of the circle of twelve states gradually lost its popularity. Somadeva refers to only nine states : neutral state, intermediate state, ambitious state, enemy of ambitious states, rearward enemy, rearward friend, rearward enemy's friend, rearward friend's friend and hilly tracts between the ambitious state and its enemy. In the commentary on the *Nītivākyāmṛta* (A.D. 1484) only seven types of states, including the intermediate hilly kingdom, figure.[66] The *Bārhaspatyasūtra* speaks of only three types of state : hostile, friendly and neutral, but it is not exactly in the context of the *Maṇḍala* theory. *Caṇḍeśvara*[67] also does not include the twelve types of states in the theory, which he has discussed summarily.

The *Saptāṅga* theory of the state first formulated by *Brahmā* in his original code or *Nītiśāstra* and then propounded in the epic acquired greater popularity during the times of Kauṭilya (*c.* 300 B.C.), Manu (*c.* 200-100 B.C.) and when *Yājñavalkya* and *Viṣṇu Smṛtis* were compiled (*c.* 100-300 A.D.) by their respective disciples, and further during the period : *c.* 300-900 A.D., when some of the *Purāṇas*, *Smṛtis* and *Śukranīti-sāra* dealing with this theory were composed. Keeping in view the largeness of the state and the necessity of protecting it different rules were framed and elaborated by the political thinkers about its seven constituents on the strength of which its existence and growth depended. The king being the central pillar of the state and its heart and soul or the brain of the body-politic had not only to protect himself from all dangers but all other six organs of the state, which were all inter-linked. Actually, the state was only the means through which the king had to achieve the end, which was the attainment of *dharma*, *artha* and *kāma*.

Kāmandaka[68] also ended his explanations of the seven constituents of the state with this observation that the stability of the whole state is based on *Kosha* or resources, *bala* or army and on the efficiency of ministers, but its ultimate goal is to attain *dharma*, *artha* and *kāma*, called *param-trivarga* in the *Mahābhārata*.

The comparative and relative importance of all the seven constituents of the state were assessed by Kauṭilya and his predecessors (different *ācāryas*). But the fact remains that no element excelled others. The importance of each element was judged, according to the changing political situation, the fluctuating fortunes of the rulers and the nature of relationship, which they maintained with the neighbouring kings. All the elements worked unitedly and harmoniously since the epic age. Their organic unity has been greatly emphasized in the epic.[69]

NOTES & REFERENCES

1. *Manu.*, VII, 208.
2. *Yāj. Sm.*, 1, 352.
3. Kullūka, *Manu.*, VII, 206-7.
4. *Mbh. Śānti Parva*, 308, 153-55.
5. *Ibid.*, 118, 27; 119, 19 f; *Mbh. Udyoga Parva*, 36, 35-37; 122, 20-26.
6. *Mbh. Śānti Parva*, 69, 19.
7. *Ibid.*, 69, 22.
8. *Ibid.*, 92, 35.
9. *Mbh. Āshramavāsika Parva*, II, 1.
10. *Mbh. Śānti Parva*, 69, 16; 162, 17-25; *Agn.* 239, 34-37, 40-43; *Kām. Nīti.*, 4, 75-77.
11. *Mbh. Śānti Parva*, 84, 23 and 34; 162, 6-16.
12. *Mbh. Karṇa Parva*, 64, 27.
13. *Mbh. Śānti Parva*, 81, 3.

14. *Ibid.*, 81, 4-5.
15. *Ibid.*, 81, 6.
16. *Agn.*, 239, 35-37.
17. *Kām. Nīti.*, 4, 71 and 74.
18. *Ibid.*, 8, 56; *NVA.*, 29, 33-34.
19. *Arth.*, VI, 1.
20. *Mbh. Śānti Parva*, 87, 30.
21. *Ibid.*, 69, 28.
22. *Ibid.*, 69, 16, 32-38.
23. *Mbh. Udyoga Parva*, 91, 10-11; *Karṇa Parva*, 81, 7.
24. *Arth.*, VI, 2; *Kām. Nīti*, 8,56; *Agn.*, 223, 21-22; *Viṣ. Dh. Pu.*, 2, 145, 15-16.
25. *Agn.*, 225, 9; 233, 21; *Viṣ. Dh. Pu.*, 11, 65, 18; 11, 175, 15.
26. *Kām. Nīti*, 8-56; *NVA.*, 29, 33-34.
27. *Mishra*, B.B., *op. cit.*, p. 191.
28. *Mbh. Śānti Parva*, 59-70.
29. *Mbh. Āshramavāsika Parva*, 11, 1-6.
30. *Agn.*, 233, 11-13. See the whole chapter.
31. *Mbh. Śānti Parva*, 59, 70; 69, 64-68; 108, 2-3; *Āshramavāsika Parva*, 11, 1-12.
32. *Agn.*, 233, 11-26; 240, 1-4; *Viṣ. Dh. Pu.*, 2, 145, 11-16; 2, 150, 3-5.
33. *Arth.*, VI, 2; VII, 1-18.
34. *Manu.*, VII, 156-168 and 169-210; *Yāj. Sm.*, 1, 345-48; *Vis. Sm.*, 3.
35. *Kām. Nīti.*, 8, 20-41, 56 and 86; 9, 2-18.
36. *NVA.* pp. 311-43.
37. *Raj. Pr.*, pp. 31-330.
38. *RNM.*, pp. 44-46.
39. *Manaso.*, pp. 94-116.
40. Kane, P.V., *op. cit.*, pp. 689-92; N.N. Law, *Aspects of Ancient Indian Polity*, (Oxford, 1921), pp. 195-208. The present author regrets his failure of having access to his book, *Inter-state Relations in Ancient India*, London, 1920.
41. *Arth.*, VIII, 1.
42. *Ibid.*, VI, 2; VII, 1.
43. *Manu.*, VII, 156-168, 169-210.

44. Quoted in *Kām. Nīti.*, 8, 22 and 41.
45. *Kām. Nīti.*, 8, 20-41.
46. *Daśk.* ed. by Godbole, (Bombay, 1917), 8, p. 104.
47. Kane, P.V., *op. cit.*, p. 691.
48. *Mbh. Śānti Parva*, 69, 64-68; *Mbh. Āshramavāsika Parva*, 11, 5-7; *Agn.*, 234, 16-20; Ch. 240; *Viṣ. Dh. Pu.*, II, 50, 2-5; *Arth.*, Bk. VI and VII; *Manu.*, Ch. VII, Kālidāsa (*Raghu.*, 8-21) also refers to *Shādguṇya*; *Pdm.*, *Svargakhaṇḍa*, 38, 61-64.
49. *Mbh. Śānti Parva*, 69, 64-68.
50. *Mbh. Āshramavāsika Parva*, II, 4-6.
51. Thapar, Romila, *From Lineage to State* (Bombay, 1984), p. 156.
52. *Mbh. Śānti Parva*, 69, 32-38.
53. Roy, B.P., *op. cit.*, p. 339.
54. *Kām. Nīti.*, 9, 2-19; also B.B. Mishra, *op. cit.*, pp. 194-95; *Agn.*, 240, 6-13.
55. *Agn.*, 226, 5-6; 241, 46-63.
56. Roy, B.P., *op. cit.*, p. 338. *See also* U.N. Ghosala "The System of Inter-state Relations and of Foreign Policy in the early *Arthaśāstra* State", *Ancient India*, pp. 137-138.
57. *Vāl. Rām.*, (Gorakhpur, V.E. 2040), VII, 62, 18.
58. *Mbh. Śānti Parva*, 34, 31-34.
59. *Arth.*, 7, 16.
60. *Manu.*, VII, 202-203.
61. *Agn.*, 236, 22.
62. *Yāj. Sm.*, 1, 342-43; *Viṣ. Dh. Sū.*, 3, 42 and 47-49.
63. *Rāj. Pr.*, p. 111 (based on the statement of Kātyāyana).
64. *Manu.*, VII, 32; VII, 68; IX, 312.
65. *Mbh. Āshramavāsika Parva*, 9, 15.
66. *NVA.*, 29, 20-29.
67. *RNR.*, p. 59. For details see B.B. Mishra, *op. cit.*, pp. 192-93.
68. *Kām. Nīti.*, 4-77.
69. *Mbh. Śānti Parva*, 69, 63; 308, 155-56.

GLOSSARY

Technical Terms and Unfamiliar Words Used in the Work

(In English Alphabetical Order)

Ācārya :	The Chief among the political thinkers, preceptor or propounder of a theory or doctrine, serving as a beacon-light for his successors.
Adhikaraṇas :	Departments.
Adhikāriṇs :	Ministers with portfolios or the heads of deptts.
Adhirāts :	Great rulers.
Adhisvara :	Sovereign rulers.
Adhyakṣa :	Departmental head.
Ādiṣṭa :	The offering of land.
Adṛṣṭanara :	One who used to make an agreement with enemies.
Agra-Mahāmātra :	The foremost minister.
Ākrandasāra :	An ally of a king ruling over the state near a hostile king.
Āmantraṇa Pariṣada:	An Advisory Council.
Amātyamukhya :	Prime-Minister.

Amātyas : The chief among the ministers or the most faithful and loyal ministers to the king.

Anantara : An immediate neighbour belonging to the category of an enemy.

Anaya : The failure on the part of the *amātyas* to make arrangement for treaty.

Aṅgas : Limbs, organs or constituents.

Anikasthas : Incharge of elephants.

Antapāla : Minister incharge of frontiers.

Antarvaṅiśika : The chief officer looking after the domestic affairs.

Anu-sāmanta : Officials working under *Sāmanta*, who was the chief of one hundred villages.

Apanaya : The failure on the part of the *amātyas* to repulse the constant attacks of the enemies.

Arājaka Rājya : A state where anarchy prevailed in absence of a king.

Arājaka Rāṣṭra : A state where there is an anarchy and despotism.

Ari : The hostile king living in the neighbourhood of a powerful king.

Ari-Mitra : An ally of a hostile king.

Ari-Mitra-Mitra : Friend of enemy's friend.

Artha : Resources, opulence.

Arthaśāstra : Science of polity.

Āsana : Neutrality.

Āstavarga :	Eight subjects.
Astrācārya :	Incharge of weapons.
Ātamiya :	Friends.
Atāvika-Force :	Tribal rulers ruling over the forest kingdoms.
Ātmā :	Own army.
Audaka-Durga :	A fort surrounded by water on all four sides looking like a delta.
Āyudhāgāra :	Magazine, an armoury or arsenal
Bala :	Armed forces or army.
Balādhyakṣa :	General of the army.
Bhajamāna :	Ancestral or traditional.
Bhaujya :	Feudatory state.
Bhoja :	In Southern India the Kings after coronation were also known as *Bhoja*.
Bhupati :	One of the titles of the king.
Brāhmans :	The priestly class who took an active part in state politics as advisors of the king.
Briddhi :	Growth.
Cakravartirājā :	A sovereign ruler or a ruler whose sovereignty was acknowledged by the neighbouring kings.
Chhina :	At the cost of fertile land.
Daṇḍa :	Army or law.
Daṇḍakartā :	Those kings who enforced the law.
Daṇḍanīti :	A comprehensive code of law.
Daṇḍanītiśāstra :	The science of polity dealing

especially with law.

Daṇḍa-Pāla : The officer-incharge of the maintenance of the army.

Daṇḍaśāstra : The *Śāstra* dealing with war strategy, law, etc.

Daśādhyakṣa : The chief of the ten villages.

Daśagramādhipati : The chief of the ten villages.

Dauvārika : The chief officer functioning as a door-keeper of the palace.

Deśa : A territory or particular region forming part of the state.

Dhanusha : Yards used in term of distance.

Dhānvana-Durga : A kind of fort constructed in a secluded place surrounded by desert.

Dharmā : Law and duty.

Dharma-Mahāmātrās : Officers-in-charge of law or *dharma*, justice and morality for bringing about material and spiritual good of the people during Aśoka's time.

Dharmaśāstra : The *Smṛti* literature.

Dharmasthāniya : Civil court.

Dharmātmā-mitrā : The righteous friend.

Divyāvadāna : The Sanskrit Buddhist text.

Dravya-Prakṛti : Each of the twelve kings had five different elements. Thus, 12x5=60 were considered as *Dravya-prakṛti*.

Dronamukha : A block consisting of four hundred villages.

Durga-Adhyakṣa : The head of the deptt. of forts.

Durga-Pāla : The officer-incharge of the forts.

Durgas : Forts and fortifications.

Duṣṭasāmanta : The hostile feudatories.

Dūta : The minister of diplomacy.

Dvādaśarājamandal : A confederation of twelve kings.

Dvādaśarājika : A circle of twelve kings ruling over twelve different types of state.

Dvaidhibhāva : Duplicity or dual policy.

Dvairājya : The state jointly ruled by two kings.

Ekarāts : Sole rulers.

Gaṇa : A corporate body, an association or a group of the republican community. The term also signifies the republic itself. It denotes the form of govt. run by the whole community together without any king or chief.

Giri-Durga : A fort on the mountain or surrounded by mountains on all sides.

Gopas : Village officers.

Grāma : The smallest unit of a *janapada* or a village.

Grāmādhīpati : The chief or headman of a village.

Grāmādhyakṣa : The chief of a village.

Grāmini : The head of the village

corporation or chief of the village.

Gṛhapati : Chief of the family.

Gupti : Defence.

Harem : A place where girls of perfect beauty were kept for sexual enjoyment.

Jala-Durga : A fort constructed on the bank of river or a fort surrounded by water on all sides.

Janapada : A territorial unit comprising both rural and urban areas with the people.

Janapada-Nivāsi : The people inhabiting a *janapada*.

Janapadavāsi : The inhabitants of a territorial unit.

Janghākārikas : Those who earned living in far-flung areas.

Jātis : Castes.

Kāma : Sex-matter, or desire of sensual enjoyments.

Kantakaśodhana : Criminal court.

Kapāla : An equal.

Kārmāntika : The officer-in-charge of the mines and factories.

Karṣa : A silver currency.

Kasbā : A branch town.

Kharvatika : A block consisting of two hundred villages.

Kosha : Treasury or resources.

Koshādhyakṣa : Head of the treasury.

Koshāgriha :	Treasury-house.
Koshthāgara :	Store-house.
Krosa :	One *Krosa* equivalent to 2 miles.
Kṛtasambaddham :	Friends acquired through matrimonial relationship.
Kṛtayuga :	*Satayuga*.
Kṛtrima :	Artificial friend or a friend won over by offering something.
Kṛtrima Śatru :	Always hostile to others.
Kṣatriyas :	Warrior kings who protected the people of the state according to the established rule of law and justice.
Kṣaya :	Decay.
Kula :	Family.
Kulapatis :	Chiefs of the families.
Kulas :	Plots of land.
Kullam :	Plot of land with fixed area.
Kulya :	Ancestral.
Madhyama :	An intermediate king occupying a territory close to both the conqueror and his immediate enemy.
Mahābalādhikrita :	War minister or chief of the army.
Mahajanasammata :	The name of a king, according to the Buddhist account.
Mahāmātras :	Provincial rulers of Asoka's time.
Mahāprachaṇḍa-daṇḍanāyaka :	The minister or officer-in-charge of war.

Mahārājā : A great king.

Mahārājya : A great state.

Mahi-Durga : A fort made of stones or bricks.

Maitrasambaddham : Friendship established on the basis of matrimonial relationship.

Maṇḍala : A group of friendly, hostile and neutral kings.

Māndalika : An officer enjoying the status of a feudatory chief.

Mantra : Policy.

Mantri-Parishad : Council of Ministers.

Mantri-Parishada-Adhyaksha : The president of the Council of Ministers.

Mantrins : Ministers.

Manuṣya-Durga : A fort protected by all four wings of the army.

Mātsya-nyāya : A particular state of justice, according to which the bigger fish swallowed the smaller ones.

Mitra : Allies or friends.

Mitra-Mitra : Friend of a friend.

Mitra-rāṣṭra : An allied group of friendly states.

Nagar-Dvāra : Gates of towns or cities.

Nagaras : Towns or cities.

Nartaka : Dancer.

Naṭa : A group of people expert in performing different arts and games had their settlements in the state capital. Their chief occupation was to amuse the king and his associates through acting, dancing and other miraculous deeds.

Nāyaka : Chief Army Officer.

Nibandhakāras : The composers of treatises on *Dharmaśāstra* and *Rājanītiśāstra*.

Nigama : A corporate association or guild of merchants.

Niṣkuhadvāra : Wall with holes.

Nītiśāstra : The Science of polity.

Nṛpati : One of the titles of the great king.

Nṛi-Durga : A fort protected by the people.

Nyāyādhisa : Chief Justice.

Oṛasa : Ancestral or descendants of kith and kin.

Paṇḍita : Minister of law or *dharma* and morality.

Paradūsana : The offering of all the land produce.

Param-Trivarga : *Dharma, Artha* and *Kāma*.

Parambhattāraka : One of the epithets of those kings who considered themselves as representatives of Gods.

Pararāja : Others' state.

Paribhūṣana : The offering of all the land produce.

Paricchada-Amātyas : Ministers of native origin, learned, wise and loyal to the state.

Parikramā : The offering of money to protect one's kingdom.

Parikrama : The signing of treaty after offering money to protect kingdom.

Parkiya : Others.

Pārshnigraha : An enemy who suddenly attacks the conqueror.

Pārshnigrahasāra : An ally of *pārshnigraha*.

Parvat-Durga : A fort made on the mountains.

Paura : The people of *pur, nagara* or capital city.

Paura-Janapada : The Assemblies of the capital city and the *janapada* respectively or the people of the *pur* and *janapada* respectively.

Paurāṇic : Based on the evidence of the *purāṇic* literature.

Prādeśikas : Officer-in-charge of a division or a provincial Governor.

Pradeṣṭa : Officer-in-charge of issuing proclamation.

Pradhāna : Premier, president of the council or the chief of the whole administration.

Prādvivāka : Minister of Justice.

Prajā : Subjects.

Prākṛta : A friendly king living adjacent to the frontiers of neighbouring king.

Prakṛta-Śatru : Neighbouring hostile king.

Prakṛtis : The seven constituents of the state; people's representatives dealing with various subjects, etc. It also denotes the number of kings and the number of elements possessed by them.

Praśāsta : Minister-in-charge of prison.

Praśāstri : Officer-in-charge of prison.

Pratikāra : Mutual help, retaliation, retribution or counter-action.

Pratinidhi : Representative.

Prithvipati : The king whose *janapada* or *pura* was rich and prosperous and well equipped with happy and contented subjects and faithful ministers.

Pura : *Nagara* or capital city.

Purāṇa-kāra : The writers of the *Purāṇas*.

Puravāsi : The inhabitants of *nagara* or capital city.

Purohita : Priest or the minister of religion.

Purusāntara : Chiefs of the armies.

Rājā : King.

Rāja-Prakṛti : The confederation of twelve kings equivalent to 12 *prakṛtis* was collectively known as *rāja-prakṛti*.

Rājadharma : The duties and functions of the king.

Rājaduta : Minister of diplomacy.

Rājakṛts : King-makers.

Rājamandal : A confederation of kings.

Rājan : *Rājā* or king.

Rājanagari :	The state capital.
Rājanitiśāstra :	The Science of polity.
Rājaśāstra :	The Science of polity.
Rājaśāstra-praṇetārah :	The *ācāryas* or preceptors who expounded the theories or doctrines relating to the state and govt.
Rājukas :	Revenue settlement officers or ordinary provincial governors.
Rājya :	State or kingdom.
Rājyabhumi :	The territory of the state.
Rājyaśāstra :	The polity relating to the state and govt.
Rājyavāsi :	The inhabitants of the state.
Rakṣita :	He who is protected from danger.
Rañj :	To please the people.
Rāṣṭra :	The territorial unit, a *rājya* or state.
Rāṣṭrapati :	The ruler of whole *rāṣṭra* or state.
Rāṣṭravāsi :	The inhabitants of the *rāṣṭra*.
Rāṣṭrikas :	The people of a *rāṣṭra*.
Rāṣṭriya :	The ruler.
Ratnins :	King-makers, and creators of *rājya* or state, which was placed in the hands of a particular king.
Sabhā :	An assembly.
Sabhāsadas :	The members of *sabha* or an assembly.
Sabhātthaka :	*Purohita* or minister pleni-

potentiary.

Sabhāyas :	Ministers with portfolios.
Sabhya :	The Advisory Council.
Sachivas :	Ministers or counsellors.
Ṣādgunya :	Six-fold stages of diplomacy.
Sahaja :	Natural friends.
Sahaja Mitra :	Friends obtained through near relatives.
Sahaja-śātru :	Enemies found among own relatives.
Sahārtha :	Undependable allies.
Sahāya :	Helper.
Sāhayāh :	The assistants employed by the king.
Sahāyas :	Ministers, *amātyas* or colleagues.
Śākhā-Nagara :	Branch-town.
Samāhartā :	Tax-collector.
Saṁgha :	A confederation of repbublican states, republican corporation, etc.
Saṁgrahaṇa :	A block consisting of ten villages.
Saṁgrahita :	Treasurer.
Samiti :	The council—a larger body than the *sabhā*.
Saṁkhyāyakas :	Clerks.
Sāmrājya :	An empire.
Samrāta :	An emperor.
Saṁsraya :	Seeking shelter or a weak king seeking protection of a stronger king.
Samudaya :	Source of income.

Saṁyoga :	Joint venture to achieve some aim.
Saṅaddha :	Very close associate.
Saṅdhi :	Alliance or treaty.
Saṅdhivigraha :	Peace and war.
Saṅgata :	Friendship.
Saṇṇidhāta :	Treasurer or *koshādhyakṣa*.
Saṇṇidhātri :	Minister of treasury.
Saphitajanapada :	Prosperous *janapadas* or state.
Sapta-Prakṛti :	Seven limbs of the state.
Ṣaptātmaka-Rājyam :	A state with seven constituents.
Sārvabhauma :	Sovereign.
Śatādhyakṣa :	Chief of a hundred villages.
Śatagrāmādhipati :	Chief of a hundred villages.
Śataghnitopa :	Cannons with hundred mouth.
Śatru :	Enemy.
Śatru-rāṣṭra :	Hostile state.
Senāpati :	Commander-in-chief.
Shāḍgunya :	Six-fold policies relating to diplomacy.
Shrotriyas :	A class of *Brāhmaṇas*.
Skandhopaneya :	Shoulders of servants.
Smṛtikārs :	The authors of *Smṛtis*.
Sṛenis :	Guilds or an association of merchants and traders.
Sthānikas :	Officers designate for looking after *nagaras*.
Sthāniya :	A block consisting of eight hundred villages.
Sthāniya-Nagaras :	Headquarters of 800 villages.

Śudras :	The fourth social order.
Suhṛda :	Well-wisher.
Sumantra :	Minister of finance or treasurer.
Sūtrakāras :	The composers of the *Sūtras*.
Svāmīn :	The king.
Svarājya :	Self rule or an independent state.
Svarāṣṭra :	Own *rāṣṭra*.
Svarāta :	The title of the kings in the Western India.
Trivarga :	Growth, decay and *Sthān*.
Udāsina :	Neutrality or indifferent attitude.
Upagraha :	Purchasing safety of life at all cost.
Upahāra :	Gifts.
Upanyāsa :	To achieve something good.
Uparājā :	Representative of a king.
Uparīka :	Provincial rulers.
Upāya :	Ways and means or expedients.
Upekṣā :	Indifference.
Vairājya :	A kingless state.
Vaiśyas :	Traders, representing the third social order.
Vaṁśakrāmanugāmi :	The hereditary line.
Vana-Durga :	Fort constructed near thick forest.
Varnāṣrama-Dharma :	The allotted duties of the four *Varṇas—Brāhmaṇas, Kṣatriyas, Vaiśyas* and *Śudras*.
Vigraha :	War or hostility.

Vihāras :	Place for enjoyment.
Vijigishu :	Conqueror or a powerful king seeking conquest.
Viṁsāḍhyakṣa :	Chief of the twenty villages.
Vi-rāt :	Kingless.
Virāṭa :	One of the titles of the king, particularly the mighty one.
Viśas :	The representatives of the people, a community or tribe.
Viśaya :	A territory.
Viśayapatis :	District administrators of the Guptas' times.
Viśpatis	The chief of the *viś* or tribe having settlement.
Vyāpārādhyakṣa :	Officer-in-charge of trade and commerce.
Vyasaṇa :	Deviation from the right path.
Vyāvahārika :	Practical or pragmatic.
Yajñaśālā :	A place where *yajñas*, sacrifices or religions ceremonies were performed.
Yāna :	Expedition or march of the army.
Yojana :	One *yojana*=4 *Krosa*.
Yuktas :	Subordinate officers-in-charge of the revenues of the king or codifiers of orders in the office of the *Mahāmātras* during Aśoka's time.

INDEX